In Data We Trust

In Data We Trust

How Customer Data Is Revolutionizing Our Economy

*Björn Bloching, Lars Luck
and Thomas Ramge*

BLOOMSBURY

LONDON · NEW DELHI · NEW YORK · SYDNEY

First published in Germany in 2012 by Redline Verlag as *Data Unser*

Original German copyright © 2012 Redline Verlag, an imprint
of Münchner Verlagsgruppe GmbH, Munich, Germany

First published in the United Kingdom in 2012 by

Bloomsbury Publishing Plc
50 Bedford Square
London
WC1B 3DP

www.bloomsbury.com

Bloomsbury Publishing, London, New Delhi, New York and Sydney

A CIP record for this book is available from the British Library.

ISBN: 9-781-4081-7951-2

This book is produced using paper that is made from wood grown
in managed, sustainable forests. It is natural, renewable and
recyclable. The logging and manufacturing processes conform
to the environmental regulations of the country of origin.

Design by Fiona Pike, Pike Design, Winchester
Typeset by Hewer Text UK Ltd, Edinburgh
Printed and bound by CPI Group (UK) Ltd, Croydon CR0 4YY

For Katrin.

For Maren and my father.

Once more for Anne.

Contents

Introduction

'I suspect that when the history is written two hundred years from now, a trend will emerge as something very important that happened in human thinking during the time when we were alive, and that is that we are becoming rational, analytical, and data-driven in a far wider range of activity than we ever have been before.'

Larry Summers, former President of Harvard University and chief economic adviser to Barack Obama

Beer and Nappies

There were harbingers of the customer data revolution in the early 1990s – on the shelves of Wal-Mart's stores, among other places. The world's largest retailer had invested early in database systems, initially in order to optimize its logistics and warehousing. A number of anecdotes circulate about how the company's marketers had their eureka moment regarding information technology. A Wal-Mart manager told us it happened like this: a smart cookie on the board never tired of stressing that in the databases' jumble of information there were unbelievable treasures, of which no one had yet dreamed. He convinced his colleagues to set up a competition with substantial prize money. Two people in the IT department started to sift through billions of lines of receipt data to find surprising correlations. And what do you know? From early evening onwards, beer and nappies often ended up in the same shopping trolley.

It's not hard to find the psychological triggers behind this purchase pattern. Men on their way home are not thrilled by the thought of soon having to change nappies, so they reward themselves in advance. The two IT workers suggested placing beer offers next to the nappy shelves in future. Test markets showed that impulse purchases shot up. And this simple but effective marketing measure of 'shelf optimization' was introduced in all stores.

The beer and nappies example is now 20 years old. Back then, only a few large corporations had the resources for data mining – in other words, the intelligent analysis of structured data sets. The technology is more democratic now. Today, any pizza delivery service can use databases to improve customer retention. The more advanced users know what their customers are willing to pay and have an approximate idea of what and how much they purchase with the competition. Google, Amazon, Apple, eBay and Facebook have built their global business models on (customer) data. They and their all-conquering information point to where things are going in the realm of comprehensive customer knowledge and differentiated communication.

Whales in the Sea of Data

This book tells the story of the data that companies gather about us and use in customer relationships. Its story should interest all of us, and not just in our role as customers. The customer data revolution is part of a larger change. After the personal computer and Internet, digitalization has now reached a third stage. Data storage is becoming ever cheaper, data processing ever faster and the algorithmic software that analyzes the data is ever more intelligent. Information scientists have dubbed this revolution 'Big Data'. The data sets are growing exponentially. We are just learning how to use informational raw material in all areas of life. Data is the stepping stone to a new level of understanding; Big Data will change society, politics and business as fundamentally as electricity and the Internet did. At the renowned science and technology university ETH Zurich, Dirk Helbing, the physicist, mathematician and sociologist, is building a machine that could be straight out of a sci-fi novel. The trend scouts Matthias Horx and Holm Friebe say that Helbing's 'Live Earth Simulator' is the 'most ambitious prognostics project since the Oracle of Delphi'[1]. The world simulator aims to calculate the epidemic path of the swine flu virus through a real-time analysis of the growing mass of relevant data. It will identify effective measures to fight climate change and set off alarm bells if another financial crisis looms. Used for business, the simulator will be able to calculate whether a product's introduction will make life difficult for the competition – or cannibalize sales from the company's own portfolio of products.

Wired magazine's founder Kevin Kelly sees the Internet as a 'magic window'. Only little children had dreamed that such a window would ever exist. IT systems in the era of Big Data can do what IT visionaries foresaw decades ago. They can collect the knowledge of the world on a screen. They spot connections that are too complicated for people to grasp on their own. And they form models that use calculations of probability to give us a window into the future. Computers know us better than we know ourselves – or at least, they are often more reliable than we are at saying how we will behave in certain situations. Based on our customer profile, car hire companies know how much petrol will be in the tank when we give the car back. An analytically driven online retailer knows the probability of a regular customer buying something at a certain

---

1 'The World Simulator', *Trend Update* 10/2011.

price. And the retailer will know how much has to be invested in personalized advertising in order to make the sale. Credit card companies can predict with a high degree of success which couples will divorce in the next five years.

There is no lack of data with which to measure reality. Nor of business-relevant data. The smartphone has removed the distinction between the online and offline world. It translates our day into a stream of data. Digital payment systems are ever more popular and bring purchases out of the anonymity of the bricks-and-mortar world. Businesses themselves leave ever more digital tracks and so become increasingly transparent in business-to-business markets. At the same time, we are learning to recognize patterns in the exabytes (that is, 10 to the power of 18 bytes) of publicly accessible data, for example in the relationships on social media, where the motto could be 'show me your friends and I will tell you who you are'. We can use these patterns for 'predictive modelling', in order to calculate the probable behaviour of groups and of individuals. The idea might not be one we are fond of, but as consumers we are predictable.

The value of data grows when it is linked up. If this happens in real time, the door to a new age of customer interaction is opened. The era of intuition is over. Not only can IBM information technology beat the human all-time champions in answering ironic, trickily formulated general knowledge questions on the cult US quiz show *Jeopardy!*, but when IT has access to the right customer data, it also sells better than the experience and gut instinct of marketers. And that's not someone's opinion; it is empirically provable. *In Data We Trust* will prove it with hard figures and case studies. Our aim is to support business decision-makers and interested consumers as they navigate an age in which data is the 'glue' in customer relations.

SAP's CEO Jim Hagemann Snabe describes the challenge of data mining and business analytics in our age of huge data quantities as the need to find 'the needle in the haystack' in real time. A marketer well-versed in IT put it nicely when he said, 'We have to find the whales in the sea of data'. If the authors of this book had to condense its message into a single word or slogan like a classic ad, then we would say: 'Crunch! Crack the data sets!' Your own and the easily available ones floating in that sea! If you don't do it, others will. Analytically driven companies know the markets they can address much better than those businesses that don't work their data sets hard; they can segment their target groups more appropriately and they are able to interact with customers in a more personalized way as they know their customers' needs.

Data-based marketing offers businesses a wonderful opportunity of becoming more intelligent than the competition. In 10 years' time, at most, it will be seen as a matter of simple 'hygiene' for customer data to be gathered and evaluated intelligently. In other words, companies without this capability *will disappear from the market*. And moreover, customers can now crack the data too. Checking a price comparison app on your smartphone as you stand in front of a shelf is just the start.

The Evidence of Evidence

There has never been a more interesting time to work in marketing and sales. For the first time in the history of mass-market selling, we are able to look inside the head of each individual customer. A 360-degree view of the customer has long been a wish of sales and marketing teams, but today, if we link up data intelligently, a deep understanding of individual customers can now become real. We are no longer asking small focus groups, as traditional market research did, 'What did you think of this product? Which product would you like to have?' We are finally moving from the role of the questioner to an observer's perspective. The aggregated data points allow us to measure customers' behaviour and from that to draw the right conclusions about the four great marketing Ps: Product, Price, Place and Promotion. Data-driven marketing – or data marketing for short – allows us to communicate the right offers in the right way at the right price to an individual customer at the right time. When added up, knowledge of every individual customer also means that we have a much more accurate bird's eye perspective of the whole marketplace, including market potential and the interesting segments of the market.

The superiority of evidence-based management is becoming ever clearer. A comprehensive and methodologically excellent study under the direction of Erik Brynjolfsson of the MIT Sloan School of Management came to the following conclusion: companies with data-driven decision-making processes increased their efficiency by 5 to 6 per cent[2]. Data-driven marketing is an important sub-trend in this development – probably the most important one. In a world where the creation of value is modularized, innovations can (unfortunately) be kept exclusive for only a limited time. The world is flat. Technology, processes and business models are copied mercilessly. Products and services are becoming increasingly similar. The technology executives of an important car manufacturer once expressed it like this: 'Today we are all the same under the bonnet.' Banks and insurance companies provide white-label services. Who, in a blind-tasting, will notice the difference between a market leader's jam and

---

2 Brynjolfsson, Erik, Lorin Hitt and Heekyung Hellen Kim. 'Strength in Numbers: How Does Data-Driven Decision-making Affect Firm Performance?', April 2011. Downloaded from http://executive.mit.edu/resource/documents/StrengthinNumbers.pdf.

a discounter's own brand? If it is hard for consumers to distinguish between products, knowledge about the customer is one of the most important competitive advantages businesses still have. And to look at it from the other side of the coin, knowledge of what is done with our data should be part of everyone's general education.

In Data We Trust – in a Nutshell

Data marketing does not make current marketing methods obsolete; rather, it harnesses them and uses analytics to develop them further. Our story about data and customer relationships starts in the corner shop. In Part I, we will show that a small shopkeeper could do many things without the aid of systems that today's mass-market companies are only just realizing are possible again. For example, he knew his customers and could serve them personally. He practised customer relationship management on a scribbling pad or in his head. His friendly words for everyone were much more customer-centric than the massive temples to shopping were in the second half of the last century. As the mass markets of the Western world were slowly becoming saturated, and as societies were becoming more diverse and consumption needs ever more individual, producers and merchants started to realize that pushing an unending wave of products with ever louder traditional advertising no longer had the same impact. Companies needed to approach customers in different – and differentiated – ways.

In the 1980s, by which time all large companies had mainframe computers in their basements for book-keeping and inventory purposes, US banks and airlines achieved their first successes with the newly dubbed 'database marketing', soon to be called 'customer relationship management' (CRM). As so often in the history of information technology, the new systems promised much and started promisingly – but the realization of plans proved difficult.

Many companies burned holes in their pockets trying to get closer to customers via data. Data analysis turned to data paralysis. The disappointment was as great as the hopes had been. CRM became a curse. And at roughly the same time, the so-called 'New Economy' collapsed.

Enter the second generation of online users. They had a built-in connection to data, while the technology start-ups had their own natural interest in using such data in competition against offline companies. Social media gave this development a turbo boost. In online worlds suddenly much was possible – 20 years after the IT industry had prematurely said new ways of working would 'not be a technical problem'. Companies with offline backgrounds can learn a lot about understanding customers from the digitally driven newcomers. Part II of *In Data We Trust* describes how to do that.

First, we will develop a theoretical model of how all marketing and sales executives can obtain a considerably better understanding of the individual customer. We will also map out the interrelated effects of this when applied to an understanding of the whole market. We call this model the 'market mosaic'. The aim is to work with smaller and smaller 'mosaic tiles' in order, ideally, to obtain an HD-sharp 'picture'.

In Chapter 2.2, important case studies show how organizations can gather focused insight into their customers' behaviour. Even though many of the best practices come from business-to-consumer (B2C) markets, we also look at the potential in business-to-business (B2B) markets. There is a simple reason for this. When considering the use of data for marketing purposes, the focus is normally on consumer relationships. However, in our experience, in the B2B sector the data seas' whales are often easier to catch. This is because the necessary data is often more readily available in companies' or public databases, and so the restrictions relating to data usage are considerably fewer and competitors are often – as far as data analysis goes – still playing in the amateur league. In many industries, competitors have not even started analysing their data yet. The competitive advantage of B2B companies that start data crunching can thus be correspondingly high. Chapter 2.3 shows how and why evidence-driven companies put themselves to the test every day; how they measure success (and failure) and constantly develop new tests to generate evidence that is fundamental to their strategic and operational decisions. In this context, we will also look closely at an acronym that no marketer will soon be able to avoid: ROMI – the Return on Marketing Investment. Smart marketers know that if the ROMI is right, the activity (and budget) will survive the next marketing crisis.

In Part III, we look at three groups whose support is essential for the success of data-based marketing. They are the workforce; marketing service providers and partners; and customers. Staff need to understand that the intelligent use of customer data is a condition of meeting the rising expectations of customers. For sales and marketing departments, the positive side-effect of being the departments with the best understanding of the customer is that they move straight to the centre of the organization. Traditional partners in the marketing process – for example, market researchers, creatives, media agencies, IT service providers – all have to be tied into the data marketing process in new ways. They also have to equip themselves with new methods of analysis. New partners, such as social media analysts, will also need to be involved. Finally, there is the largest challenge of all: customers have to at least tolerate data marketing and, if possible, love it. If the marketing feels like spying, then obviously the company has shot itself in the foot. The data does not belong to the marketer but to the customer, and right-thinking companies will not stray into murky legal waters even when the frontiers of the data world are not always adequately policed. There is no need for a moral appeal here. It is a matter of self-interest, because customers are more powerful than any data protection agency.

Nobody Wants to Be a Nobody Now

In the coming years, a consumer culture will develop along the lines of a list of the conditions according to which most customers are willing to share data with companies. The data-marketer has to create a sufficiently transparent and safe framework. Customers have to see the value of it and consider that the use of the data is appropriate. We all know that trust is hard to gain and easy to lose, and this is particularly true for the commercial use of personal data. The companies to profit from the customer data revolution will be those that respect the rules of this new consumer culture, build trust – and prove they deserve it.

No one today can predict where consumers in future will draw the line regarding privacy. There will be areas where we keep an extremely close eye on the potential for our data to be misused. And there will be areas where we are more relaxed about the information we share, because the advantages far outweigh the danger of misuse. In current discussions about data use, the sceptics and regulators set the tone of the debate. The advantages and opportunities to both providers and consumers are often neglected in these exchanges. *In Data We Trust* casts a realistic eye on what is technologically possible and economically sensible regarding the commercial use of customer data. Customer trust is the necessary foundation to all of these suggestions. However, we are considerably more confident in the competence and learning curve of users than we are in that of the loudest voices in today's data protection debates.

Most enlightened consumers share their data voluntarily and consciously – and not because they are tricked into it by loyalty card administrators or social networks. Loyalty card users – many of them signed up long before the Internet came along – receive a discount or special offers. Facebook users, often 'digital natives', use a technological platform for social interactions that are important to them. Neither group is made up of sheep that need to be protected from the data wolves. They draw their own lines around public and private spheres. No one is forced to use a loyalty card or Facebook profile. Of course, there is the danger of data being misused. The wisdom of the mass of users will, in the medium term, force the provider of data-driven services to play by the users' rules. Among other things, this means clear and easily understood opt-in and opt-out functions when private data moves into the public digital domain.

Sceptics and regulators are holding on to a strangely idealized image of anonymity in public space. The majority of people want to be themselves online *and* offline. People want to be addressed by their own name. They use the name in their passport for customer reviews. They have no problem about telling the world what their relationship status is; nor must their mobile number be as secret as MI5's.

The Internet's age of 'masks' is over. No longer will people camouflage themselves like Odysseus in front of the Cyclops. Second Life, the online world where people used avatars, brands advertised on virtual billboards and retailers had digital shops, was the Internet flop of the last decade. Today, people want to be themselves. They want to be found. A growing group of consumers is sharing data out of conviction and with enthusiasm. The blippy. com platform provides an insight into what self-chosen transparency can look like. When a member of the community pays for a product by credit card, the social shopping platform automatically publishes the location, price and time of the purchase. The default setting for consumption is public, as the network user's friends can benefit from this information. For marketers and sales people, it means this: enlightened consumers are open for dialogue with companies. Many even seek actively after dialogue. Marketing and sales need to seize this chance – in order to get to know customers better. And in order to predict their consumption moods. And, ideally, in order to know their wishes before the customer even knows that he or she has them.

Part I

The Customer, That (Un)known Quantity

Don Draper Is Dead – The Limits of Traditional Marketing

'This device isn't a spaceship, it's a time machine. It goes backwards, and forwards . . . it takes us to a place where we ache to go again. It's not called the wheel, it's called the carousel. It lets us travel the way a child travels – around and around, and back home again, to a place where we know we are loved.'

Don Draper (in the *Mad Men* TV series) about the legendary Kodak Carousel, the slide projector with a circular tray

CRM in Your Head

The choice in a three-year-old's play-shop is somewhat limited. Plastic fish, wooden vegetables, a few drawers of basic foodstuffs, corned beef and tinned tomatoes. Nevertheless, a few fresh herbs have made their way from the kitchen to the wooden shelves. The ritual begins, 'Good morning, sir. What would you like? I have delicious fish and corned beef.' Sir doesn't like corned beef. He takes two fish and the three-year-old pipes up immediately, 'You'll need potatoes too. And parsley, or the potatoes won't taste nice. OK?' Only a killjoy would say no. 'That's £30.'

The friendly little shopkeeper lives on in children's bedrooms. And so do the strengths of a local shop: a nearby location; a close personal bond; an ability to give suitable advice – and high prices. The child's play-shop takes us back to the understandable, friendly and personal consumption of times gone by.

Of course, small shopkeepers cannot do everything better than Wal-Mart, Tesco or Sainsbury's – they wouldn't have been banished to a business niche by the supermarkets otherwise. (Even though the concept of the small 'convenience store' has had a minor renaissance, driven by a few chains.) A brief analysis of the retailer-customer relationship in traditional small-scale structures can, however, highlight a few obvious truths of good marketing which mass-marketing professionals may have forgotten

In the four Ps of Sales – Product, Price, Place and Promotion – the shopkeeper has an advantage in at least two areas. His proximity (Place) to not very mobile customers in busy urban districts was the basis of his original success. Much more important, however, is his Promotion through personal bonds to his customers and recommendations. The local grocer and his wife probably knew every regular customer and could talk to them as individuals. A good greengrocer remembered which kind of apple a customer prefers. And he reminded the customer when a fresh batch of that variety came in. He knew which new products he could suggest to which customers with a good idea that they would be convinced to buy. One-to-one marketing was around long before the concept was coined. Indeed, the shopkeeper was even able to make on-the-spot decisions about extending credit or not.

Even regarding Product, the comparison between a local shop and a supermarket with 30 brands of lemonade on offer is not as simple as our current ideas about the obvious superiority of variety might suggest. Feedback helped the grocer to match his selection at least to certain groups of his customers. And if he matched them well, then word-of-mouth marketing helped to increase his catchment area. Only on Price could the local grocer never compete.

The bottom line is that on a small scale, the grocer had many of the things large retailers are dreaming about today. His good knowledge of his customers meant that he had good data about them – even if his customer database existed only in his head, backed up by handwritten notes. He was able to pay attention to individual wishes, which led to a high degree of customer loyalty. Long before target-group marketing, CRM and the digital world's economy with its *Cluetrain Manifesto*[1], he knew that markets are made up of individual customers and that you retain them best by talking to them individually.

At the heart of the grocer's business model is a highly up-to-date understanding of the need to focus on the customer. The clever grocer did not think along the lines of quick sales and low margins, nor did he calculate the turnover for each of his wares. He saw the value of a customer in the profit which can come from a long-term customer relationship. Or, formulated in actual marketing terms, he was aware of the variables that relate to success: 'customer life-time value' (the total value of a customer over the length of the business relationship) and 'customer equity' (the value of the customer to the company's future revenue). As we now know, that was not enough. Personal selling at the counter is a great thing. But giving advice to each individual can lead to high staff costs and little room for scalability. According to studies by the British anthropologist Robin Dunbar, most people can maintain social relationships with about 150 people.[2] Admittedly, 'Dunbar's Number' will vary from person to person – a good grocer, like good networkers – will take the number up to 200 or 300. But someone's head is a cognitively limited CRM system.

---

1 www.cluetrain.com
2 Dunbar, R. I. M. 'Coevolution of neocortical size, group size and language in humans', in *Behavioral and Brain Sciences* 16 (4), 1993, pp.681–735.

'Pile It High. Sell It Low'

The first hints of the supermarket revolution came in 1916. In Memphis, Tennessee, the entrepreneur Clarence Saunders asked a simple question: Do people actually always have to serve people? His answer was Wiggly Piggly, the first shop to make a point of self-service. His franchising system, with its standard shop floors and national marketing campaign, soon made Saunders rich. In the 1920s, The Great Atlantic and Pacific Tea Company (or A & P for short) won market share from small competitors with a similar concept. Incidentally, one of the largest challenges to self-service shops was shoplifting. However, the costs of security measures were less than the costs of giving personalised advice to customers. This new breed of shops did not sell meat or fresh produce. According to the US Food Marketing Institute's definition, the first 'real' supermarket with a full range of products opened on 4 August 1930 in a garage in the New York district of Queens. With 560m^2 of shop floor, the King Kullen store used the slogan 'Pile it high. Sell it low'. Its space was divided by product type. Large product packs sold at discount prices attracted a great number of families and a large car park prefigured the shopping habits of the post-war suburban lifestyle. Six years after the first one opened, there were already 17 King Kullen stores in New York.

World War II briefly slowed the rise of the supermarket to its position as the most popular destination for everyday shoppers. After 1945, a number of social and technological trends converged across the Western world. These would prove difficult for small shopkeepers to counter.

- The growing affluence of the middle class led to a rapid increase in buying power.
- Electrical fridges and freezers became mass-market products.

- First in North America and then in Europe, cars became the habitual beast of burden for the weekly shop on the edge of town.
- A growing number of women went out to work, and were keen to stock up on non-perishable convenience food, of which the supermarkets had a larger selection.

The supermarket was both the consequence and forerunner of mass consumption. In 1948, Migros in Zurich opened the first European supermarket. [3] The age of marketing for the masses, who were driving growth, had begun on the other side of the Atlantic too.

Marketing and the Good, Old World of Advertising

Don Draper has it easy. At least as far as sales go. The hero of the *Mad Men* TV series is selling in the growth markets of the 1960s. His agency comes up with campaigns for products which many people do not have, but really want to have. The manufacturers produce series of innovative products whose technological superiority is easy to portray in print, radio and television ads. They set the pace for the marketers and advertisers. Whoever has a freezer will soon need a microwave.

Consumer society is still relatively homogenous, as is the media landscape. Market research has a minor role, now and then delivering customer type profiles. The main character's gut instinct and creative genius are of decisive importance. In short, Don has it easy because a traditional campaign has limited wastage in mass markets

---

3 König, Wolfgang. *Kleine Geschichte der Konsumgesellschaft: Konsum als Lebensform der Moderne* (A Short History of Consumer Society). Wiesbaden: Steiner, 2008.

with homogenous strata of buyers. In addition, consumers are not yet able to fast-forward through the ads that come on during their favourite TV programmes.

In Western Europe, the markets were to some extent even more homogenous than in the US. Families with traditional concepts of roles formed the backbone of society. The main cohorts accounted for 70 to 80 per cent of society. The destruction wrought by World War II was followed by reconstruction and with it came enormous demand. Until the 1970s, 'sales' consisted of supplying people with wares according to their needs at the time. In other words, in the post-war years people had to meet their basic needs first. Then, during the economic miracle, many people had the means to enjoy luxuries and indicate their status with products. The car became a central symbol.

From small shopkeeper to data-based marketing

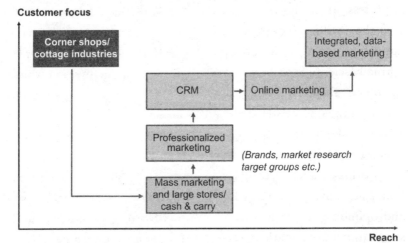

Before the 1973 oil crisis, marketing was in essence about providing guidance in the context of a growing variety of products. Its guiding question was this: how can I ensure that given the boom in consumption, as many customers as possible hear about our product and can also obtain it? In growth markets, the ability to deliver the product well is a strength. Everywhere. Immediately. Coca-Cola showed everyone how it could be done. Wherever and whenever someone thirsty wanted to be part of the American dream, all she or he had to do was run to the nearest kiosk or vending machine.

Don Draper and his gut instinct were just the start. Over the course of the TV series, he becomes an advertising fossil. That accounts for the series' popularity with advertisers. His gut-instinct marketing arouses nostalgic feelings, just like his much-cited interpretation of the Kodak Carousel as a time machine that takes us back to a place where we know we are loved.

The Professionalization of Gut Instinct

The more mature the markets became, the more marketing needed to professionalize itself. Large networks of agencies sprang up all over the world. They supplied ever more brands with creative campaigns (some more creative than others). Today, it is not normally scientists or engineers who decide which products reach customers. Business studies quickly grew in importance, though, and from the mid-1970s the business faculties of universities were sending a growing number of young people who had at least gained a theoretical knowledge of marketing and sales out into the corporate world. Parallel to this development, the market researcher's hour had come. They had taken on methods from social research and opinion polls, such as in-depth interviews and group workshops (qualitative market research) and panel studies with questionnaires (quantitative market research). The retail trade optimized lines of sight and directed shoppers' paths through stores, as well as introducing point-of-sale offers. Towards the end of the 1970s, marketing and sales became increasingly important elements in companies' strategic decisions. Long-term marketing goals were created. Institutional change followed functional change. In the 1980s, many marketing and sales departments received their own high-level management.

The professionalization of marketing has changed the world of consumption. It has made brands big by deriving the brands' values from society's values, which in turn served individual desires. For example, Marlboro was associated with freedom. Market research has helped separate out more defined target groups, allowing (for example) to offer the Mini to women motorists with good salaries in urban areas. It has given us amusing campaigns that create sympathy for, and encourage attention to, new brands. At the same time, the campaigns had to become ever more innovative and targeted. Now, however, that no longer works – or if it does, it comes at a horrendous price.

Inflation on All Channels – Attention Is Becoming Increasingly Expensive

'Half the money I spend on advertising is a waste. The problem is, I don't know which half.' This observation by John Wanamaker, the father of modern marketing, is today often answered by online marketers: 'Now we know: it's the half for TV ads.' It's a good line, but a little exaggerated. TV is still one of the most effective forms of above-the-line advertising. However, the essence of the answer is true: a traditional campaign in moving images is a shadow of what it once was. In the US 20 years ago, a large manufacturer could reach 80 per cent of the population with a TV ad on the three main TV networks. Today, he has to run a campaign in dozens of media channels in order to reach the same numbers. According to the market research company Carat, expenditure on TV advertising will continue to rise in the near future. At the same time, it will become more difficult than ever to reach individual consumers. The cost per 1,000 television viewers has risen by about a third in the last decade even though customer response is not encouraging. In some mature economies, over two-thirds of advertising campaigns are unable to substantially increase either turnover or market share.

Television is only the tip of a melting iceberg. Traditional advertising's effect has been sinking for years. That is no secret among marketers. The causes are as varied as they are far-reaching:

- Multiplication of the customer segments: we live in very heterogeneous societies. What campaign can speak to single mothers and young-at-heart senior citizens, to DINKs (Double Income No Kids couples), to homosexuals, status-oriented hedonists and digital natives? All at the same time? None.
- Multiplication of products and brands: globalization has added a new dimension to choice. No matter how small the niche, there will be a sub-brand out to get it. Soon, older people will no longer recognize the brands of car their young relatives drive.
- Multiplication of media channels: as our access to a wider range of TV channels has increased, so the Golden Age of advertising has come to an end. In the 1970s and 1980s, the early evening ads on ITV in the UK were known to all members of the family, from Smash mashed potato to Shake 'n' Vac carpet cleaner. The inflation in advertising time through Channels Four, Five, and subsequently the Freeview and cable stations inflated the value of a TV ad. At the same time, the newspaper and magazine market was becoming more differentiated. The number of radio stations

dramatically increased and as if all of that was not confusing enough, Tim Berners-Lee invented the World Wide Web.

- Multiplication of competition: the number of operating businesses that have a strategic approach has also increased. That means there are more competitors with the support of professional agencies fighting for the attention of potential customers. However, the number of customers is not increasing in the saturated markets of the Western world.
- Multiplication of the sales channels: the Internet and online retailing have messed up the old marketing mix. How can you advertise when location is no longer important and prices are completely transparent? Few have yet found a definitive answer that does not originate online.

The decreasing efficiency of advertising reveals a further weakness of traditional advertising: the Return on Marketing Investment (ROMI) is measured only indirectly or not at all. The typical figures like audience reach, price per thousand contacts etc. measure the activities but not their effect. Which customer really bought as a result of which activity often remains hidden. No wonder that in times of economic crisis the marketing budget is often the first to be cut.

Ignoring the Ads

The increased complexity of the markets, media landscape and sales channels is just one facet of the current crisis in marketing. Another one is consumers' defensive reactions to advertising. In the early 2000s – the Internet was just starting to establish itself as a serious advertising medium – a small silver box called 'TiVo' shocked advertisers and advertising agencies in the US. TiVo was one of the first hard disk recorders to systematically filter out ads.

And it was the technological expression of a growing social phenomenon. Thousands of advertising messages rain down on us every day. We have learned to avoid them both consciously and unconsciously. At least, that is what 60 per cent of German consumers say. And if not, we are like the three-year-old shop-keeper in his bedroom when he hears the message 'Tidy up!' – it goes in one ear and out the other. Only 12 to 13 per cent of television viewers can remember a TV ad.[4] In a historical perspective, this means that the gold rush of the advertising agencies in the 1980s and 1990s ended up over-stretching target groups' ability to pay attention. Nor is this just a phenomenon for the big brands with mass-media campaigns.

For one of our projects, we talked to an office supplies retailer about advertising activity. Meticulous bar charts showed how often he had used which advertising measures to inform his customers of his offers. From the customer's perspective, there was not a single day in the year when she was not ambushed by at least 15 advertising measures. The office supplies retailer is a good example of how marketing tends to fall into the inflationary trap of its own measures. Some of the marketing measures have grown historically. In the case of this retailer, this took the form of his complete catalogue, which has all the charm of a telephone direc-tory. Smaller advertising titbits for important, normal and less important (A, B, C) as well as new and lost customers are used to 'complement' the catalogue. His response rate to mailings is low, typically just 1 or 2 per cent. This not only increases the insecurity of the marketing department, but also the number of mailings. That is not an isolated case but a typical 'prisoner dilemma', as a

---

4 'Was Werbung treibt – Kaufmichjetztichdrückdich!' ('What advertising pushes us to do: buymenowI'mtellingyou'), *brand eins*, 5/2006.

games theorist would say. Every retailer knows that less, but more focused, advertising would be better for everyone. But out of fear that the 'advertising pressure' from the competition could be stronger, everyone carries on as before. To formulate it somewhat drastically: in spite of a much-vaunted need to be customer-centric, advertising today is the logical continuation of mass-market communication. It is centred on the product and on selling the product in the largest possible volume. The customer and his needs become so marginal that no one asks the banic question: does the customer want all of this?

Is traditional marketing over?

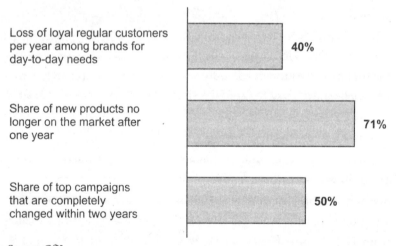

Loss of loyal regular customers per year among brands for day-to-day needs	40%
Share of new products no longer on the market after one year	71%
Share of top campaigns that are completely changed within two years	50%

Source: GfK

The customer does not need to be asked. The answer is expressed in their increasing perception of products as interchangeable. Banks, telecom companies and energy companies fight hard – and with some success – to stop customers drifting away (the so-called 'churn rates'). But when the price and offer are no longer right, then the customer goes – in spite of, or because of, rising marketing budgets. The number of advertising messages washing over consumers is rising. Today it is already around 3,000.[5]

The End of Market Research As We Know It

Let's quickly summarize the state of marketing. While people in the 1990s would watch TV programmes that collected the top ads from around the world, most customers today are fed up with them. Their taste and their needs are becoming ever more differentiated. They are faced with a vast selection of products and brands and they make use of the wide range on offer. Here and there one brand, like Apple, manages in grand style to awaken desires that consumers did not even know they had and such companies' products allow customers to feel they are the pioneers of a larger social revolution. In Apple's case, that revolution is the complete digitalization of the world in its aesthetically most appealing expression. For the majority of brands, the new complexity creates one thing above all: cluelessness.

It is, of course, well known that there is one profession that is paid to know consumers' needs. Unfortunately, traditional market researchers have the same problem as traditional advertisers. They often do good work – and cancel each other out. Their interview methods become more refined, their panels larger and their data sets more specific. And indeed, particularly the quantitative data from TNS, Gallup, Kantar, GfK and such companies does provide a way in to data-based marketing approaches. Yet just like traditional advertising, traditional market research has today reached the limits of its methodology. If everyone knows the same thing, then not even the most detailed of analyses provides a competitive

---

5 From 'Kein Geld verschwenden' ('Don't waste your money') in *acquisa*, 06/2010, pp.34–35.

advantage. This is really a logical consequence of recent economic history.

Market research coupled with traditional advertising has led to a scale-up in volume markets. Admittedly, detailed follow-up to customer surveys has led to one or two major flops, like the Ford Edsel and New Coke. But for the most part, market researchers knew a lot. Which district with what purchasing power still had space for an electronics store, for example? Which retail brand had what potential to keep its price-sensitive customers happy? However, market research has not (yet) got to grips with the increased individualization of the markets.

Here is an example from our consultancy. Recently we were asked to supply customer profiles based on market research data for a large car manufacturer. These profiles were to be the basis for the brand portfolio, the design of new models and the associated marketing strategies. We very quickly came to the conclusion that the basic data was insufficient in two ways. Firstly, all the major car manufacturers have access to the same basic data, so it would be extremely difficult to derive a really superior marketing approach. Secondly, the data set says nothing about potential customers who may once have been in close contact with the brand but then plumped for a different car in the end. Just where the data could have been interesting, it was either unable to answer such questions or was prohibitively expensive. Which takes us back to the local grocer again. He knew which customers left his shop with empty shopping bags.

The Corner Shop Scaled Up

Marketing has to reinvent itself. There is broad consensus about this, but marketers' vision of themselves in the future is surprisingly one-dimensional. Everyone wants to appropriate the techniques of social media marketing, push their budgets into Internet marketing, 'better integrate' the diverse channels of communication and offer more opportunities for interaction. And that is about all that an uncertain profession is offering. Of course, these ideas are not all wrong. But botching together an advertising plan for Facebook is not the answer. The current methods of online advertising will be obsolete as quickly as an annoying radio ad. Perhaps even sooner. Email advertising very swiftly moved from its promise as the future of direct mail to being spam mail. Reinvention is something else.

Market research and marketing have to scale up the local shopkeeper. Or to be more specific: in our diversified mass markets, we have to get to know the individual customer as well as the local grocer knew his customers. Marketing and sales will need to reinvent themselves if we are to be as personal as a corner-shop owner in how we react to customers at every possible point of contact, the so-called 'touch points', while also offering a much wider range of products with much more intelligent pricing. A large European telecom provider has made a good start. In a pilot project, it has sifted through all available customer data. That allows a sales assistant in the shop to identify a customer – and without having met the customer before – to greet him, for example with this: 'Hello, Mr White. Your contract runs out in two months. We'd like to keep you as a customer and so we have the following offer for you. . .' Naturally that works only if we use all available data points – in this case the contract data coupled with usage data, face recognition and the evaluation of the user's Internet browsing behaviour. In that way, we can make mass markets transparent and controllable on the level of the individual customer.

In a Nutshell

- Small shops were highly customer-centric businesses. They were able to react to customers' individual wishes. Grocers' shops knew long before the *Cluetrain Manifesto* that markets are made up of conversations.
- In 1930, the first 'real' supermarket with a full range of wares opened in New York. After 1945, social and technological trends converged on the entire Western world in a way that threatened small shopkeepers: women worked, fridges became commonplace and society became mobile thanks to the car. The first European supermarket opened in Zurich in 1948.
- There was limited wastage from traditional marketing campaigns in growth markets with homogenous strata of buyers. In addition, consumers had not yet learned – or were not yet able – to filter out the advertising messages they were exposed to. Thus, until the first oil crisis, marketing was in essence about providing guidance in the context of a growing variety of products. Its key question was this: How can I ensure that, given the boom in consumption, as many customers as possible hear about my products and can obtain them?
- The saturation of markets meant the challenges for marketing increased. From the mid-1970s, a large number of young people were leaving university and beginning work with a theoretical understanding of marketing and sales. Parallel to this development, the market researcher's hour had come. They had taken on methods from social research and opinion polls, such as in-depth interviews and group workshops (qualitative market research) and

panel studies with questionnaires (quantitative market research). This meant marketing could target groups more specifically. And marketing helped to make customers enthusiastic and loyal to companies.

- In all sectors, the efficiency of traditional advertising has been plummeting for years. The most important causes are: the multiplication of customer segments, of products, of brands, of media and sales channels as well as the increase in international competition in a globalized world.
- So marketing and sales teams need to scale up in the way that a small shopkeeper works. In other words, in our diversified mass markets we must get to know the individual customer just as well as the local grocer knew his customers.

Data Overload – Six Lessons CRM Hype Has Taught Us

'There are 10 types of people: those who read binary code and those who don't.'

A geek joke (1 followed by 0 in binary code is 2)

CRM: Hype or Curse?

The story of data-based marketing has many highs and lows. Or to put a positive spin on it: it is a story full of learning experiences. In the 1990s, the letters 'CRM' (Customer Relationship Management) attracted a lot of hype. IT consultants and software companies won lucrative contracts on the back of it. Parallel to the global digitalization that accompanied the rise of the Internet, impressive early success stories started to circulate among technologically interested marketers: companies like BT, Tesco, British Airways and Barclays had been gathering customer data since the 1980s. And they had been using it systematically and successfully for telephone marketing, contact strategy optimization, campaign management and co-ordination, marketing resources management, ROMI calculations and general marketing analyses. Since the mid-1990s, the business press had been eyeing with great interest the CRM hype around companies like Oracle and SAP. Most marketing decision-makers were afraid of missing a trend that could fundamentally change the whole marketing game. IT budgets were correspondingly flexible. Sums in the two to three-digit million dollar range were the norm rather than the exception for software and its realization.

What was bound to happen *did* happen. IT hype occurs when technology in the digital world promises more than it can achieve in the short term. The dot-com bubble burst in 2001 and before long, CRM had turned from a magic word into a curse. Too many companies had set up too many data cemeteries – and buried too much money there. The figures revealing low usage of advanced IT tools for marketing purposes speak for themselves. This is even true of US companies that are traditionally open for IT innovation. Mark Jeffery, director and IT expert at the Center for Research on Technology and Innovation at Northwestern University's Kellogg School of Management, presented the following results in a recent survey of 252 companies with a total marketing budget of US$53 billion:

- 57 per cent of companies have no central database for tracking and analyzing their own marketing campaigns
- 70 per cent do not use Enterprise Data Warehouses (EDWs), i.e. a central storage facility for their data, in order to collect their customers' interactions with the company or its marketing campaigns
- 71 per cent use neither EDW nor other tools to choose and design their marketing campaigns
- 80 per cent do not use an integrated data source to undertake automated, result-based marketing measures (e.g. sending birthday wishes)

In order to use CRM systems effectively, companies have to do more than equip themselves with IT tools. The right technology is just one of the preconditions of a successful CRM operation. Firstly, the management has to come up with a rigorous strategy, outlining what goals are aimed for with which customers using which means.

This is particularly true of B2B markets, where the relatively easy access to customer data means that data-based marketing can lead very quickly to successes. (We will look at this in detail in Chapter 2.2.) At the same time, structures in the organization have to be changed: if the right structures aren't in place, often there will be no capacity or capability to provide individual service to those carefully identified customers. And finally, there is also the issue of corporate culture. If staff are not customer-focused, all the marketing efforts will be in vain. Once these preconditions have been met, frictionless processes have to be implemented in order to identify customers individually, take full advantage of all potential opportunities, keep them loyal and then measure the success of these activities from all angles.

How the management of individual customers in CRM can fail due to complexity

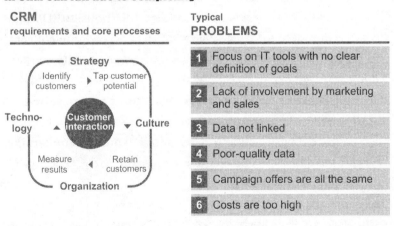

CRM
requirements and core processes

Strategy
Identify customers
Tap customer potential
Technology
Customer interaction
Culture
Measure results
Retain customers
Organization

Typical
PROBLEMS

1 Focus on IT tools with no clear definition of goals

2 Lack of involvement by marketing and sales

3 Data not linked

4 Poor-quality data

5 Campaign offers are all the same

6 Costs are too high

Many companies are scared off by this complexity. Unhappy memories of past, flawed IT projects often influence their decisions. However, that is no reason not to pursue data-driven activity. Lessons need to be learned systematically from past mistakes. Again and again during our projects, we have come across six typical problems (see p.35). One of the most common derives from the attitude that the first thing to do is to collect lots of data . . . and *then* see what to do with it. That is a sure path to data overkill.

IT first?

Of course, we are strategy consultants and so are convinced of the key role of strategic planning in IT-driven marketing, as elsewhere. Naturally, you could say our perspective is subjective. In many projects that have stalled or failed by the time we are called to look at them, we have seen the following common traits.

A company has a fairly complex IT landscape. Customer-relevant data is stored in a number of databases. The company's marketers feel they could open up new market potential with cross-selling marketing campaigns. The company has collected data on transactions, bonus programmes, product usage, service and complaints. Yet the marketers soon realize that in the current IT structure, the data that they need for cross-selling – such as potential-related data and transactions data – cannot be filtered out of the various areas. They ask the IT department how it can be done and are told, 'We have to consolidate our IT landscape once and for all'. Consolidation always sounds good. The marketing director and the director of IT then together try to convince the Chief Financial Officer (CFO) that this investment is urgently needed. This is where most projects falter, due to the high costs, long time-frame for implementation and uncertain potential for application. If they do not end here, the CRM project will start – but often on the wrong footing. An enthusiastic Chief Technology Officer (CTO) wants to make her mark and takes charge of the project. The Chief Marketing Officer (CMO) likes that – he does not have the time or inclination to get his head round complex data worlds. The sales department is invited to all the meetings too, but the sales managers feel they have even less time than marketers – after all, they have to go out and sell. The ambitious CTO builds her ideal database in her head. It is at the cutting edge of what is technologically achievable. She writes a set of comprehensive technical specifications.

The project is then prepared in three time-consuming steps:

1. All the available data is collected.
2. All the processes in the company are documented.
3. The state of the ideal IT infrastructure is derived from the previous steps.

If everything seems to make sense, then the programming begins. The decisive question of what key information is needed for the company to generate profitable growth is often asked too late. The worst case scenario is high investment costs without useful applications, a great deal of frustration and the realization that those practical Excel tables did the job pretty well in the first place. This analysis might sound like a caricature. Our perception is that in many IT projects – not only in marketing – it represents the bitter reality and has the fatal consequence that in data-based innovation often the baby is thrown out with the bathwater.

Critical to the success of nearly all projects with data components is the need to form a cross-functional unit drawing together colleagues from IT, marketing and sales. The unit must see itself as a team, and have a common language.

Tech-speak, Marketese and Sales Jargon

AT&T's marketing department had taken on a mammoth task for the 2001 season's Super Bowl. The NFL final is also the yearly showdown for US advertisers. Many big campaigns start with an ad aired between kick-off and the last touchdown. If possible, that ad should make advertising history. The most expensive ad agencies' quarter-backs throw their balls as far as they can. In that year, AT&T stood out for their conspicuous modesty: a white background against which you could read the URL www.mLife.com. It cost US$20 million to broadcast. Of the 100 million Super Bowl viewers, unfor-tunately a few too many went to the website at the same time. The server collapsed. Almost no one found out that 'mLife' was a new mobile phone offer, let alone that it had anything to do with AT&T.[1] The ad went down in advertising history as both a classic blunder and as a strong reminder that marketers and IT people need to talk to each other – a lot – as soon as information technology plays a role in marketing activity.

What percentage of the big IT projects run according to plan? (By that, we mean within the planned time-frame and the allocated budget.) The figure the IT analysts The Standish Group came up with is 28 per cent.[2] The blame for failed IT projects quickly falls on IT departments in most organizations. It is an easy conclusion to draw and the phrase 'IT departments' says it all. As we sketched out above, it is often the CTOs and IT project managers who like to take control. Or to put it another way: those in positions of respon-sibility in marketing and sales often shirk their responsibilities and then complain afterwards that nothing works or has a useful appli-cation. The technology for data-based marketing is far too impor-tant to be left to technologists, says Mark Jeffery. We can only agree – but also add one thing: sales and marketing people have to learn to collaborate better on data-based marketing activity.

---

1 Jeffery, Mark. *Data-Driven Marketing. The 15 Metrics Everyone in Marketing Should Know*. Hoboken, New Jersey: Wiley, 2010, p.228.
2 Ibid, p.234.

Techies, marketers and sales people not only speak different languages, their worlds are also based on different thought structures. Techies want what is technologically possible and do not always think in terms of results. Marketers are often analytical people. They think in terms of complex customer typologies and want to know as much as possible about customers so that they can optimize their marketing mix. Hard drives are cheap, so they ask IT to 'please save as much data as possible'. Sales people want to sell. As quickly and much as possible. Their immediate attention is drawn to the low-hanging fruit, the easy deals. Complex analyses often seem bothersome to them. The language barriers are comparatively easy to surpass. Their differing thought structures are a bigger problem.

The Silo Mentality and Data Repositories

When a regular guest arrived in a leading luxury hotel 10 years ago, the receptionist would pull out a small file card. On it would be all the important data about him: marital status; smoker or non-smoker; personal room preferences and his usual category of room. His breakfast or room-service preferences may have been included too. On the back was a list of his visits over the past few years. A quick glance at the card's back and front was all the receptionist needed in order to grasp all the essential information. He could address the guest in a personal way and judge the guest's value pretty accurately.

Recently, one of this book's authors was emailed a survey after checking out of a hotel belonging to a large chain. It was a dozen pages long. Among other questions, it asked, 'How did you find the table-clearing service at the breakfast buffet?' The author could just about remember the woman who served the scrambled eggs, but with the best will in the world he had no memory of how the table was cleared. We authors cannot imagine that someone without a professional interest in marketing would take the time to fill out the questionnaire. A rule of thumb is that a customer should be able to fill out a feedback questionnaire in one or two minutes at most. That is enough time in most product sectors to ask about the essential parameters. Based on this feedback, the customer can be 'processed' efficiently. In the context of data-based customer communications, the old 80–20 rule is still true, the so-called Pareto principle: 20 per cent of your data gives 80 per cent of the added value. Good systems prove themselves by their ability to filter out of large amounts of data the few really important bits of information that are relevant for marketing and sales activity.

Artificial complexity helps nobody to gain data-based access to the market. It only helps the people who sell over-complex data solutions and manage to inflate their prices because no one other than providers understands them in any detail. This creates a so-called 'lock-in', which makes it almost impossible to change provider, at least in the short term. In the long term no one benefits.

The basic rule for big IT projects is the same as that for a decision about whether or not to invest in stocks: if you do not understand the business model and/or the technology, steer well clear. Or learn about it fast. Coming back to the earlier point: data-based marketing technology is too important to be left to IT decision-makers in isolation. Marketers have to think through the system from the market's and customers' point of view, while also gathering enough technical knowledge themselves to be able to formulate the right demands at the right time. And to ask the right questions. One important question being: is there a sensible linkage of data?

Politicians have no monopoly on 'silo' mentalities. Many companies' knowledge management falls down because of them. And many data-based marketing initiatives fail because of silo structures in databases. Data repositories that are not linked are still the norm rather than the exception. Here is an example from the consumer's point of view. One of the authors was for many years a pay-TV subscriber. A highly satisfied one, at first. Yet every year the fee structure was revised and increased significantly. At some point, annoyance at the automatic price increases outweighed the pleasure in using the product and the customer sent a polite but clear letter saying that he was no longer interested in this kind of contractual agreement and would cancel his subscription if no change could be made. A standardized reply was received that the 'objection' to the new fee had come too late and the contract would run for another 12 months. The customer cancelled immediately with another reference to the automatic price rise. No reaction. Shortly before the end of the 12 months' contract, systematic customer service calls started to come from the service provider, in an attempt to win back his custom. Out of a consultant's curiosity, he talked to the call centre staff to find out what data they were basing their call on. They admitted that they had no access to information about customer cancellations. That information was in another system. That is how time and money are wasted – and turnover is lost. Ask around about contact with call centres and one key message comes out again and again: 'the left hand does not know what the right hand is doing'. In the case mentioned above, a simple linkage between databases would have been enough to increase the chances of the right approach and so also of successfully winning back the customer.

Good Data, Bad Data

Sometimes we meet companies that say, 'We don't have enough data. How can we gather more?' They are the exceptions and can often be helped relatively quickly. Mostly, marketing directors have the impression that no one in the company is any longer capable of finding – in the mess of scattered data – the relevant information that is needed to draw strategic conclusions about the market. A fragmented IT and database structure is just one of the problems. For some time now, we have observed a trend that is understandable on a human level but problematic on a business level. Firstly, companies with experience of data-supported marketing and sales measures tend to collect ever more unstructured data – for example, from social media – or to push increasing amounts of their own unstructured data on to hard drive storage, for example, the customers' interaction with the call centre. At the same time, their data hygiene is getting sloppier. It is possible to see how this is happening, as the IT industry sends the signal that its improved algorithms and greater processing power mean it can deal more effectively with large amounts of data – however unstructured they are. Or expressed in the non-techies' language: hoard all possible data and the IT crowd will crack it somehow. It is true that in-memory applications (ultra-fast calculations in memory chips) and Hadoop-based solutions (high capacity generated by linking many hard drives) are currently enabling great leaps forward in big data analysis. In the near future, they will allow analyses that were previously possible only for businesses operating in science fiction novels. Whoever wants to generate quick growth from data first has to define what he really wants and has to know. So he needs data hygiene. It will save him money and effort. Address files make for a good example.

Companies build their address lists over decades. For many companies, they are an important part of their company's value – for some, the most important part. Around 10 per cent of private addresses become invalid each year. Locations are re-named, people move, get married or divorced[3]. For B2B clients, the contact data

---

3 From 'Kein Geld verschwenden' ('Don't waste your money') in *acquisa*, 06/2010, pp.34–35.

changes just as quickly as a result of changes in personnel, company moves, re-structuring, bankruptcies etc.

Not only is this expensive (returned letters represent costs of over £1 each), but badly maintained databases of addresses with wrong forms of address, duplicates or misspelled names annoy customers. Data quality is and remains the most important factor for success in direct marketing. In-memory and Hadoop technologies are not changing that for the moment. And there are relatively inexpensive providers that update and clean up address databases; the price starts at less than 5p per corrected address. This experience with addresses is similar to that with other marketing-relevant data, whether credit ratings, information about account linkage or a history of complaints.

The same rule can be applied to data hygiene as the kitchen: the person who cleans up regularly will have less to do in the end than the person who lets unwashed dishes pile up in the sink.

Good Cards, Bad Cards

There are data-based CRM operations that seem to do everything right: they gather relevant data in a structured way and store it in sensibly constructed systems of databases. However, they still do not lead to measurable marketing success or they are so expensive to run that they cancel out any benefits derived from them. The best CRM programme is of no use if customers are wooed individually but the offers they are wooed with are interchangeable. Most loyalty cards fit into this category. Their rise began with the first CRM systems. The reality check for customers and marketing managers came halfway through the last decade when it became clear that data can cancel out other data. And that a method that starts out on a sensible basis can become so inflated and unwieldy that (almost) no one uses it any more.

At the moment, in big consumer markets such as the United States, United Kingdom, Germany and France, there are hundreds of loyalty-card-based bonus programmes all fighting for customers' attention. Analyses show that, on the whole, consumers are not prepared to actively take part in more than three bonus programmes at once. No wonder: most wallets have slots for five cards at the most – and they are filled by credit and debit cards, a driver's licence and so on. Faced with the flood of plastic cards, customer magazines, discount points and other instruments, customer loyalty programmes have now become a standard product and do little to differentiate the provider from the competition.

An example of this dilemma is the German petrol station market. DEA's participation in the multi-partner 'Payback' programme in 2000 was perceived as an indirect price reduction and disturbed the settled pricing pattern in the petrol station market. Since then, almost every oil company has introduced a customer loyalty scheme, either on the basis of loyalty cards like Total/Elf and Shell/DEA (now their own 'Clubsmart' card) and Aral (the German subsidiary of BP) or on the basis of discount points, as with Avia, Esso and OMV. The result? Possible advantage in securing market share is cancelled out, while the margins shrink due to the costs of the customer loyalty activities.

The problem with most loyalty cards is that the system offers nothing new. Secondly, it is used too infrequently, making it, thirdly, too expensive for what it does. The shopping baskets of most product categories are not big enough to make bonus values of 1 to 5 per cent attractive. One way out are multi-partner programmes such as (in the UK) Nectar and Avios. In theory, the advantage is that the customer has to have just one card, receives a more attractive programme and the wider shopping basket allows for more comprehensive analyses. There are disadvantages here too: the costs are often high, the providers have to pay a lot for the analyses and the programme can quickly come up against its limits once it has one provider from each category. A bigger problem is the incentivization of turnover that is neither in danger or capable of rising. Often this is accepted because of the loyalty card – mainly for the information that can be gleaned from it but also, to a lesser degree, for the sake of the company's image.

Data Analysis not Paralysis

A 2001 study came to the sobering conclusion that 55 per cent of all database projects do not bring any added value to turnover or profit, in spite of high costs. Often the very opposite was the case[4,5].

Whoever wanted to stay in business as a marketing and sales consultant after 2002 temporarily deleted 'Customer Relationship Management' from their active vocabulary. Even today, much of the scepticism about data-supported marketing methods stems from that time. Nor is it unjustified, as a current example demonstrates: a very large US corporation with direct sales and a strong presence in the European market invested well over €100 million in a new customer management system in the last few years. This system is still far from capable of supporting staff in the simplest of tasks. At the moment, it is not clear whether the project can still be steered in a successful direction and, if so, how many millions of euros in additional investment will be necessary. A growing number of people in the company are suggesting it would be better to make the tough decision to write off the project and its losses.

The bottom line is that there are relatively high levels of frustration

---

4 Wixom, B. and H. Watson. From 'An empirical investigation of the factors affecting data warehousing success' in *MIS Quarterly* 25 (1),'2001, pp.17–41.
5 'Der gläserne Kunde' ('The transparent customer'), *Süddeutsche Zeitung*, 28 October 2006.

around data-based marketing and data-driven customer retention. Customers have the impression that not only do companies have 'X-ray' insight into their lives, but also that the companies are unskilled at using the data. In many companies, the anecdotes about failed IT projects are water-cooler gossip. Of course, the only people who find these anecdotes funny are the people who were not directly involved and the people who seize gleefully on to them because they confirm their own prejudices. Often even large companies do not manage to find a way out of the data labyrinth, in spite of their enormous resources. And yet the software industry is doing just fine. Since the end of 2007, the market for customer management software has grown continuously and has been almost unaffected by the world economic crisis. Over US$250 billion is spent worldwide every year by companies on business software, around $10 billion of which goes on CRM software. The outlook for software companies over the coming years is rosy.

Worldwide sales of enterprise software ($US bn)

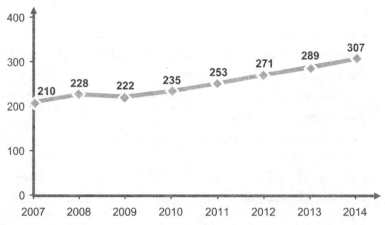

Source: Gartner

The positive trend does not come out of nowhere. Yes, generating added value for sales and marketing departments from complex data sets remains a difficult but important business. But as so often in the history of technology, new methods require some lead time before they are ready to establish themselves. It is frequently the case that new technologies come with exaggerated expectations, all linked to the flamboyant fanfares with which the IT industry tends to announce new products. Disillusionment follows soon after and people's attention dissipates as quickly as frustration levels rise. In the background, the innovators continue their work. Step by step, the technology is learning to keep the big promises made when the products first came to the market. A new phase has begun. In Chapter 3.2, we will investigate in more depth which partners and technical methods are needed to overcome the frustrations caused by the old problems of CRM tools. In Silicon Valley, there is a popular saying: 'never bet against the Internet'. It wouldn't be advisable to bet large sums against data-based marketing, either. The examples in the next chapter will provide a clear indication why.

In a Nutshell

- BT, Tesco, British Airways, Barclays and others had been gathering millions of customers' data since the 1980s. They used it in CRM systems for telephone marketing, contact strategy optimization, campaign management and co-ordination, marketing resources management, ROMI calculations and general marketing analyses. Their early successes encouraged the competition to also invest in data-based marketing.
- IT hype occurs when the technology in the digital world promises more than it can achieve in the short term. For CRM systems this was often the case.

- The right information technology is just one of the preconditions of a successful CRM operation. First, the management has to come up with a rigorous strategy. A common mistake is that at the start of the project an ideal IT infrastructure is defined. Only then does the programming begin. The decisive question of what key information is needed for the company to generate profitable growth is often asked too late.
- Critical to the success of nearly all projects with data components is the need to form a unit from IT, marketing and sales departments that sees itself as a team. The team has to speak a common language.
- People in positions of responsibility in marketing and sales often shirk their responsibilities and then complain afterwards that nothing works or has a useful application. The technology for data-based marketing is far too important to be left to technologists.
- The basic rule for big IT projects is the same as for a decision about whether or not to invest in stocks: if you do not understand the business model and/or the technology, steer well clear. Or learn about it fast. Marketers have to think through the system from the market's and customers' point of view, while also gathering enough technical knowledge themselves to be able to formulate the right demands at the right time. And to ask the right questions.
- CRM systems are once again in fashion. This positive trend hasn't come from nowhere. As so often in the history of technology, new methods require some lead time before they are ready to establish themselves. Today,

CRM systems can often do more than the industry promised 10 years ago. And they are considerably easier to
implement.

■ In the context of data-based customer communications,
the old 80–20 rule is still true, the so-called Pareto
principle: 20 per cent of your data gives 80 per cent of the
added value. Good systems prove themselves by their
ability to filter out of large amounts of data the few really
important bits of information that are relevant for
marketing and sales activity.

■ Never bet against the Internet. Nor against data-based
marketing.

The End of Intuition – Lessons Learned from the Online World

'In God we trust; all others bring data.'

W. Edward Deming

Cookie Time!

Hertz knows pretty much exactly how much petrol we will leave in the tank when we return a hire car. Online music platforms such as last.fm are remarkably adept at playing music that their listeners do not yet know and yet immediately like. And not just for a single music genre. Based on credit card transaction history, Visa is supposed to be able to predict pretty accurately which couples will divorce in the next five years – and so to draw conclusions about creditworthiness. 'Companies today can often predict your behaviour better than you yourself.' This was how Yale economist Ian Ayres, author of the bestseller *Super Crunchers*[1], described prognostic capabilities to a new generation of data-focused business intelligence experts. His book, which has been much discussed in the US, lists dozens of examples of companies that have obtained considerable competitive advantage from the intelligent gathering and analysis of data. Ayres compares the technological paradigm shift now at the start of the era of Big Data to the time of the introduction of the railways: coaches did not stand a chance once the trains came.

---

1 Ayres, Ian. *Super Crunchers: Why Thinking-by-Numbers Is the New Way to Be Smart.* New York: Bantam Books, 2008.

At the same time, the era of intuition as the basis for important marketing decisions is in its death throes. Algorithms are not only better than people at playing chess, they also know more than us about our future behaviour. This idea might not appeal to us, but clever marketers will use it. Or rather, they are *already* using it. In the next two years, marketing will change more than it has in the last two decades. As so often in the past 10 years, the online world is showing everyone the way forward.

Very few consumers have ever heard the names [1+x] Inc., Lotame Solutions or BlueKai. But these companies know us pretty well. The *Wall Street Journal* calls these companies 'cutting edge'[2], for their real-time analysis of online shoppers. The companies work for, among others, the credit card company Capital One, Wal-Mart and the electronics retail chain Best Buy. They install cookies, beacons and other online tracking systems in browsers, analyze Internet users' browsing behaviour and compare it in real time to market research data. At the same time, it is easy for these companies to find out where the computer that has logged into the Internet is located. In most cases they do not know the user's name. Nor do they need a name in order to communicate specifically with that customer.

For a thoroughly researched series of articles with the title 'What they know', the *Wall Street Journal* invited [1+x] Inc. to take a little test. Anonymous users selected by the journalists were to click just once on a test website. [1+x] Inc. was asked to recognize who had clicked on it. The data crunchers identified one user, Carrie Isaac, as a young mother from Colorado Springs with a household income of c. US$50,000 who regularly shops at Wal-Mart and often hires children's films. [1+x] knew that Paul Boulifard from Nashville works as

---

2 'The Web's Cutting Edge', in the *Wall Street Journal*, 4 August 2010.

an architect, has no children, travels a lot and buys used cars. And what about Thomas Burney? Interesting as a customer, because this man from Colorado is a construction contractor, has a university degree, high turnover on his credit card and likes to ski. His single click allowed his yearly income to be estimated at US$86,724.

'Super crunchers' show us how to do it: Fully customized advertising in real time

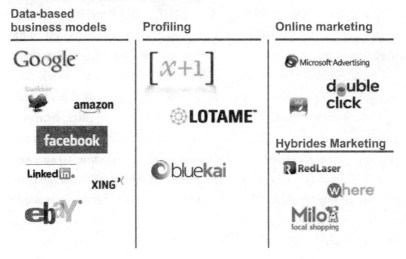

Of course, the test was more than an amusing online guessing game. Capital One uses [1+x] technology to immediately make just the right offer to potential customers. If young mother Carrie Isaac clicks on a page with a Capital One ad, she will see a standard product for customers with 'average' income and 'average' credit history. However, architect Paul Boulifard will see a 'VentureOne Rewards' offer – a card that offers double the Air Miles points for travel bookings. Contractor Thomas Burney is immediately sent to the system's top offer of a CapitalOne Prestige Platinum card. No monthly fee and no interest for a set period.

The products are allocated according to how the market researcher Nielsen sorts customers into demographic segments. Based on her digital traces in the Internet and her computer's geodata, Carrie Isaac was categorized as 'White Picket Fence'. To Nielsen's researchers this means: a consumer who lives in a smallish town, between 25 and 44 years old with at least one child, works in an office or service industry, average income US$53,901; the person has spent at least a few years in tertiary education; is normally a graduate. In Isaac's case, that hits the nail on the head. The offer of double Air Miles was also right for well-travelled Boulifard, although he could probably not have signed up, as the Nashville architect had already saved so many Miles on his American Express card that he would be unlikely to swap. Burney was also shocked by the precision of the analysis. The Capital One click put him in Nielsen's 'God's Country' segment. Such people are from the country or small towns, 34 to 54 years old, management level jobs and homeowners. Everything was right except for his age. Burney is just 28. He was successful younger than the [1+x] data analysts had supposed.

Behaviour Beats Context

It is no coincidence that the financial services provider Capital One's online marketing is at the forefront of customer segmentation. And if Capital One uses a data-based tool, then its competitors had better sit up and take notice, for the rise of the credit card bank from its foundation in 1988 to its place as a Fortune 200 company is a victory for statisticians. Or as the two founders Richard Fairbank and Nigel Morris would say, it has been a victory for 'information-based market strategy'. In the early 1980s, the two consultants had already ascertained that US banks try to find new customers with an approach that was too scattergun. They pitched their idea of individual customer acquisition based on thorough use of customer data to over 15 national banks. None of those banks believed in the power of data. One regional bank, Signet Bank from Virginia, finally gave them the chance to put their approach into practice. Fairbank and Morris sifted the Signet Bank data to identify the bank's most valuable customers (not those who repay credit quickly, but the ones who are slow to repay and yet reliable). From that data, they derived marketing measures with detailed customer segmentation. The concept was so successful that Signet soon developed its credit card business as a nationally recognized spin-off: Capital One. In its phase of aggressive expansion from 1996 to 2006, the Capital One shares grew in value by around 1,000 per cent, beating the S&P 500 Index by a factor of 10.[3] Capital One also weathered the subprime crisis relatively undamaged and is now once again on a growth course. For Capital One, the consistent use of real-time web analytics to guide communication with customers is the logical next step in the company's history.

Again, [1+x] Inc. and other data detectives working for sales do not know the customers' names. Polls show that US citizens are less sensitive about data issues than their European counterparts. However, serious online usage analysts do not look for names in the US either, although they would probably be able to find them with a high degree of success. Naturally, every user can look at all of Capital One's credit card products on Capital One's website. The *individualization* of the homepage aims to make potential customers immediately aware of an offer that is likely to match their customer profile. That will significantly increase the chance that a user will pay more attention to the offered product and not head off immediately to find a competitor site.

---

3 Davenport, Thomas H. and Jeanne G. Harris. *Competing on Analytics: The New Science of Winning.* Boston: Harvard Business School Press, 2007, p.41 ff.

In the US too, financial services providers can only make credit decisions on the basis of creditworthiness – not on the basis of age, gender, ethnic origin or nationality. Capital One is open about its use of data and so, in spite of its intensive data analytics, has never been faced with large protests about its data-based marketing and company strategies. Many customers say the individualized communication is a relief. When it works, advertising becomes information – which is when it is effective. That is exactly the point of 'targeted marketing'. This is where the business world can learn a lot from online business.

The BlueKai start-up from Seattle evaluates anonymized real-time information sent to it by cookies, Flash Player usage, Google searches or user comments. It observes an anonymized user on eBay, Amazon or Expedia, and within a fraction of a second it can deliver advertising suited to that user's behaviour. BlueKai is what the media theoretician Nicholas Negroponte always wanted with his individualized daily newspaper *Daily Me*: fully individualized advertising on a mass scale in real time. BlueKai's customers do not need to book advertising space according to general ideas like 'people buying sports shoes probably browse sports portals'. For example, Procter & Gamble now books target groups who are probably interested right now in bodycare products, because they have just posted a question about them on a forum. Or to put it another way, 'online behavioural targeting' can bring those video ads, banners and coupons to the people who will not necessarily find the advertising a nuisance.

Behaviour beats context. One of the most important capabilities of marketing that is targeted to user's behaviour is the delivery of a critical mass of advertising messages to users whose digital traces match the profile. Every message may only cost the advertiser a tenth of a cent. Yet if you deliver well over 50 million messages a day, like BlueKai, that still makes for a tidy turnover.[4] We are on safe ground when we predict that the individualization of marketing messages won't stop with banners and emails. Television and the Internet are merging, slowly but surely. With the rise of IPTV (i.e. digital television delivered using the Internet protocol), television advertising will also go down the path of segmenting customers according to their viewing habits. The set-top box will know pretty well who is watching. Someone who already owns their home will no longer have to watch five ads for mortgages during the sports show.

Big players in the digital economy have long seen that the value of marketing data is a strategic issue. In 2007, Microsoft bought the online advertiser aQuantive for more than US$6 billion and showed great interest in another giant of Internet advertising, Double Click Inc., which in the end went to Google for US$3.1 billion. One year later, Google launched its web browser Chrome, primarily in order to develop its competence in the area of web tracking. In Mountain View (where Google's headquarters are based), it was understood that the brilliant idea of simply placing Google ads next to search words (i.e. first generation behavioural targeted marketing) should now be replaced by more complicated algorithms. One thing is sure: the competition in California is not sleeping. Soon after Google Chrome appeared, Apple launched its own advertising network, iAds for iPhone and iPad, while the software factory Adobe paid US$1.8 billion in 2009 for Omniture, a specialist in return on marketing investment (ROMI) for online advertising.[5]

---

4 'The Web's New Gold Mine: Your Secrets', *Wall Street Journal*, 30 July 2010.
5 'Microsoft Quashed Effort to Boost Online Privacy', *Wall Street Journal*, 2 August 2010.

Online Data Protection

E-commerce traders and online marketers have a natural advantage in the use of data. They sell via digital systems and so have easy access to the data. Every customer who buys online has to identify him- or herself. The customer's life cycle can be tracked retrospectively from one transaction to the next, and his or her 'Customer Lifetime Value' (CLTV) can therefore be quantified with corresponding accuracy.

Our experience on many projects has taught us that tailoring communication to customers on the basis of an analysis of their data raises the response rate – i.e. the customers' positive reactions – by a factor of five, at least. In many applications, we have seen rises by factors of 10 to 20. 'Collaborative filtering', i.e. recommendation algorithms based on transactions, like Amazon's 'Customers who bought this item also bought', feels like a nostalgic memory of the Internet's early days. Targeting can do so much more now. Why? Because data can tell us so much more. Multiple conclusions can be drawn from it that go right to the heart and mind of the customer. The key to success here is that marketers compare an individual customer's characteristics with the logics of known consumer segments and derive their product suggestions from the combination of the two. The data of an online shop with good data structure can deliver this easily.

It is also necessary, as it is not only among nonconformists (who are often fundamentally critical of all advertising) that emotionally defensive reactions to advertising campaigns can be observed now. Especially in the high earners' segment, where margins are not as tight, marketers increasingly find hyper-individualized consumers. A negative response from consumers is natural when the individualization of marketing is half-hearted, as it is so often in classical segmentation or collaborative filtering that does not consider individual customers' needs. Income still correlates with education and enlightened consumers have developed a good sense of when a crude logic is being used to advertise to them. In other words, when they are not being addressed as individuals but are being made aware of products that everyone in their circle of friends already has. These are just the products they do not want, as they will wish to differentiate themselves socially through their consumption. Advanced online retailers have understood that superior under-standing of their customers can enable them to steal market share from companies that still rely on their intuition. Among the new breed are the three Samwer brothers: Alexander, Marc and Oliver.

These Berlin Internet investors made their fortune in the first dot-com bubble just before the new millennium with the eBay clone Alando. In 2008, they took a new strategic direction in e-commerce with their holding companies European Founders Fund and Rocket Internet. Their shopping sites like brands4friends and Zalando are focused on communicating with customers indi-vidually thanks to extensive data mining.

Individualized communication gains in the quality of its cross- and up-selling when customers buy at a number of online shops that belong to the same holding company and where a unified legal form ensures that all the online shops can access their affiliated shops' data. If all the customers' contracts are with the over-arching 'Customer Inc.', there can be no legal objection.

The Merging of Offline and Online Worlds

Not long ago, many offline companies were convinced that custom-ers want to talk to people, that they wanted to be given personal advice and sign contracts face-to-face. Digital communication and standardized processes were thought to be too impersonal to be truly successful. Never bet against the Internet, though. Online shops and online service providers have managed to leap across the spatial divide to their customers. In many fields, online businesses are closer to their customers than their bricks-and-mortar counterparts, even though they never see them. They get value for money and customer service right. Online businesses have learned to shape processes and interfaces in such a customer-friendly way that, today, we would often prefer to communicate with a clever machine than with a poorly trained member of staff. Traditional advertising was one-way communication: the sender delivered a message to the recipient. The Internet has created widespread dialogue for customer communication. In spite of the digital medium, it is more personal than the communication customers knew in the last century. Online communication has succeeded in making millions of customers ambassadors for brands, whether via elaborate product blogs or via the quick click of a Facebook 'like' button for their favourite brand. Especially clever providers have managed to engage consumers in customer-to-customer forums where they help each other and act as unpaid customer service.

The pigeonholes of separate 'online' and 'offline' worlds are still firmly anchored in the minds of people who were socialized before the invention of the Internet. Young consumers and the incoming generation of decision-makers in companies – people whom trend scouts like to call 'digital natives' – often no longer understand this division in people's perception of the world. In our generation, it will disappear slowly but surely. According to the research company Strategy Analytics, smartphones show strong growth and have a worldwide market share in the second quarter 2012 of 39 per cent, with some regions – such as the United States – already at 50 per cent.[6] We're now close to Mark Weiser's vision of ubiquitous computing. Until his

6 Global Handset Shipments Forecast by Quarter: 2012. Strategy Analytics (March 2012).

premature death in 1999, Weiser was a pioneering IT thinker at Xerox. At the end of the 1980s, he introduced the concept of ubiquitous electronic data processing to the debate on the future of man and machine. He then argued the case in more depth in his 1991 essay 'The Computer for the 21st Century'.[7]

Tim Berners-Lee's World Wide Web was just the ignition stage for ubiquitous computing intelligence. The mobile Internet sparked the next fuel tank. Advertising and sales will be affected like almost no other area, as the ubiquity of the computer (in the form of the smartphone) means that we can research, order and agree contracts online wherever we are, whenever we want. Our purchasing impulses will continue to be influenced by impressions that we do not acquire while we're on our own in front of our computer, but rather in the colourful physical world: when talking to friends; looking in shop windows; sitting on the bus next to a person wearing cool trainers. The first smartphone apps at the interface of e-commerce and traditional trade demonstrate the direction things are going. The RedLaser digital shop assistant is one of them.

Over 11 million users had downloaded the app on to their iPhones and Android smartphones by the summer of 2011. Its function is as simple as it is practical. Customers scan a product barcode using their phone's camera. RedLaser activates a price comparison search engine and then delivers not only comparative prices from online retailers, but also the physical addresses and prices of bricks-and-mortar retailers who have the product in stock. That sounds initially like a clear threat to traditional retail. How many shops can match the best Internet prices? Put under pressure by RedLaser, the electronics chain Best Buy shows how the app can

7 Weiser, Mark. 'The Computer for the 21st Century', *Scientific American*, 1991, p.265.

play into the hands of bricks-and-mortar shops. RedLaser under-stands not only product barcodes but also QR (Quck Response) codes. Best Buy sticks those black-and-white squares on its shelves, guiding customers with RedLaser on their smartphones to a Best Buy product page optimized for mobile Internet. On that page, they can find well-prepared information about the product in front of them on the shelf. With a further click, they can buy the product in Best Buy's online shop and have it delivered right to their house. And guess what? An Internet giant has its finger in this pie too: RedLaser has been owned by eBay since the start of 2011.

Online auctions are considered the company's bread and butter by eBay's executives in their San José HQ. However, they see the real potential for growth in the convergence of e-commerce, social shopping, online payment systems, cloud applications and the very physical shopping world in city centres and shopping malls. Goods follow data. This has been the basis for eBay's strategic investment for years. PayPal provided the initial payment application. It was intended originally as a way to simplify money transfers on eBay's own retail platform but now acts as an almost universal payment method for mobile shopping. Following the purchase of RedLaser, eBay acquired Milo.com, which gathers inventory data on around 50,000 US retail shops in real time. This includes many millions of articles stocked by the chains Target, Macy's and, indeed, Best Buy. Milo has (naturally) also integrated PayPal as the method of payment. The companies Where Inc. and FigCard complete eBay's portfolio. Where Inc. lists food outlets and retailers and shows their current special offers. FigCard equips the tills in small shops with special USB sticks that allow people to pay by mobile phone.[8]

---

8 'Wal-Mart des Internets' ('The Wal-Mart of the Internet'), *brand eins*, July 2011.

Thus, the combined data from all its systems allows an online giant like eBay, omnipresent in a consumer's shopping life, to understand customers much better than even the best loyalty card of a traditional retailer.

Reality Mining in the Cloud Economy

What does data say about customers? This cannot be answered in the abstract. The question is always dependent on context, the consistency of the data, the degree of refinement and the data crunchers' ability to find the connections that are relevant to the market. In addition, time is a factor. For easily understandable reasons, real-time analysis is the killer app for many areas of business. Anyone who does not know how to harness the immediate intelligence of the data cloud will struggle to survive.

No one can predict exactly what the effect on marketing and sales will be when the petabytes of digital information on private hard drives and isolated company databases migrate on to cloud servers. Naturally, not everyone will have access to all the data in the cloud economy either. But the amount of accessible data will grow rapidly (at least, the amount of data that can be evaluated in anonymized form). With this comes the growing opportunity to use it to predict and influence customer behaviour. Real-time geodata will come to play a key role. Alex 'Sandy' Pentland, director of the Human Dynamics Laboratory at MIT's Media Lab, introduced the term 'reality mining' to the discussion about smartphone-based location apps. Taking utmost care to uphold data protection by anonymization and consistent opt-in guidelines, Pentland is looking to find solutions that, with the aid of citizens' aggregated geodata, can bring added value to society. On a simple level, this might be to locate potholes in the, because the movement sensors in car drivers' smartphones are always shaken at particular spot. The intelligent analysis of geodata could also help to locate outbreaks of disease quickly. One of the favourite examples that the MIT computer scientist gives in lectures is that if a critical mass of residents in a certain tower block in a large city stop going out, it could point to the outbreak of a virus such as bird flu or SARS. Health officials could then react quickly and possibly prevent the spread of the virus. Pentland's company Firma Sense Networks Inc. makes reality mining accessible to companies too, including for marketing optimization.

The fine art of marketing in a cloud economy will consist of hybridizing data from consumer segments, individual behaviour and location (or patterns of mobility). Of course, respect for people's privacy is an important issue. There are still heated debates led by professional privacy advocates and the furore surrounding Google Street View is just a tiny indication of what is to come. Yet marketers discover in their pilot projects something that displeases the professional privacy advocates: responsible citizens have no problem with sharing their data with companies *if* it happens intentionally, with a defined aim and perhaps is reciprocated by small advantages such as discounts. We will look at this in more detail in Chapter 3.3.

A key message of this chapter is that, owing to the technological ease with which they can access data, marketers in online worlds have developed many methods from which B2B and bricks-and-mortar companies can learn. That is more than an opportunity – it is a precondition of future success. Or to put it more clearly: whoever does not learn from the new champions will disappear from the market. There is a simple reason for this. Since the invention of the smartphone there is no longer a separation of online and offline worlds – not for shopping, financial services, travel reservations, product development, production or supply chain management. We have to systematically research the mechanisms of data-based online companies – and make them of benefit to all companies.

In a Nutshell

- The era of intuition is coming to an end. Algorithms not only play better chess than people but companies can often predict our behaviour better than we can. 'Number crunching' will become the most important basis for marketing decisions in the next few years.
- From cleverly aggregated data points, you can draw multiple conclusions that go right to the heart and mind of the customer. The key to success here is that marketers compare individual customers' characteristics with the logics of known consumer segments and derive their product suggestions from the combination of the two. The data supplied by an online shop with a good data structure could deliver this easily.
- Behaviour beats context. 'Online behavioural targeting' is where the media theoretician Nicholas Negroponte always wanted to be with his individualized daily newspaper *Daily Me*: fully individualized advertising on a mass scale in real time. Companies no longer book advertising space but target groups that are probably interested right now in a particular product. The user will then see the video ads, banners and coupons as information rather than a nuisance.
- Big players in the digital economy have long seen that the value of marketing data is a strategic issue. They are developing their superior knowledge at considerable speed. Customer data is increasingly becoming a global commodity.

- Tailoring communication to customers on the basis of an analysis of their data raises the response rate – i.e. the customers' positive reactions – by a factor of five, at least. In many applications we have seen rises by factors of 10 to 20.
- Owing to the technological ease with which they can access data, marketers in online worlds have tried out many approaches to customers that B2B and bricks-and-mortar companies can learn from. This is more than an opportunity. It is a precondition of future success. Whoever does not learn the lessons of online communication with customers will disappear from the market.
- Since the invention of the smartphone, there is no longer a separation of online and offline worlds – not for shopping, financial services, travel reservations, product development, production or supply chain management. Data is around us 24x7. And it can be *used* around us 24x7. Advertising and sales will be affected like almost no business function, because the ubiquity of the computer (in the form of the smartphone) means that we can order and agree contracts online wherever we are, whenever we want. Our purchasing impulses will continue to be influenced by what we see in the colourful physical world rather than what we view alone in front of a computer.
- Real-time analysis will become the killer app for many areas of business, for easily understandable reasons. The fine art of marketing in a cloud economy will consist of hybridizing data from consumer segments, individual behaviour and location (or patterns of mobility).

Part II

Leveraging. Customer. Data.

The Mosaic of the Market – When We Know All the Customers, We Know the Market

'Data is the next Intel Inside.'

Tim O'Reilly

Big Data – Big Picture

Markets are made of individual customers. Big Data and the phenomena we described in Part I of this book provide marketing and sales departments with a historic opportunity. If we put data together in a skilful way, we can produce a mosaic of the market – ideally in HD quality. We will then be able to zoom in smoothly to the level of the individual pixel. And of course zoom back out again, when we need the panoramic perspective in a certain context. This HD image will give us completely new insights, ranging from the worldwide market to the individual customer and his value to the organization. Nor will we need to invent or define fundamentally new parameters or metrics for marketing. Our traditional understanding of customer value and behavioural drivers are largely sufficient in the application of data-based marketing. Or to put it another way: marketers and sales organizations do not need to do everything differently, but they need to do many things much better.

In the following pages we will outline a course of action that, based on the new data situation, is integral to an actionable market and customer segmentation. This structure will help us to recognize the value of sequences and purchasing contexts both on the level of the individual customer and in reference groups of a usefully large size. The process will ensure that we do not push customers into segments where they would not recognize themselves and that we protect them from products and advertising that they would find tiresome and that, from the offering company's perspective, is a waste of money.

First, let's step back for a moment and look at today's methods of quantitative market research and customer segmentation. If we are honest, we have to admit that in many industries and markets the mosaic of segments and those segments' behavioural patterns, even in so-called 'best practice' companies, is often only available in a granularity as broad as paving slabs – indeed, paving slabs that have not been cleanly laid but lie higgledy-piggledy on top of each other. Of course, there are exceptions, in spite of the growing streams of data, but many large companies have not managed to develop a comprehensive and consistent market understanding based on individual customer behaviour from their own customer data and other available data sources.

Let's start with a thought experiment. It is set in an Orwellian world where a true 360-degree view of the customer is possible.

Every customer always has a camera on his head and a neuro-chip inside his head. We know when he has seen what television ad and which emotions that triggered in him. We see which shops he goes into and when, which parts of the shelves his gaze rests on and for how long, and which product ends up in his shopping trolley. We know his flat and can see whether it contains an old stereo or an old sofa. We can see the brand names on the surfboards in his garage as well as the car he drives, including all its extra features. The neuro-chip tells us how much cheaper petrol has to be at Petrol Station A in order for him to make a detour of over two miles. And how annoyed he was about the price rise at the nearer Petrol Station

B that he drove past. Of course, we also know his income and all his transaction data. Name, age, gender and so on. We can aggregate every element the of individual customer data in real time and correlate it with all the data from other consumers.

The market mosaic: Understanding markets to varying levels of granularity, including on the level of the individual customer

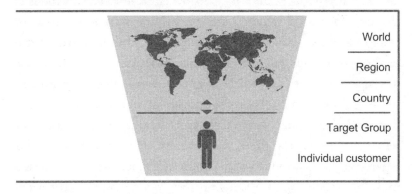

Just to make one thing clear: that imagined world is a nightmare scenario for us too. The thought experiment of a completely transparent customer is just to show what would be possible for marketers in such a consumer world. And it gives us a few indications as to which elements of that transparent world are already reality. Our smartphones track our location and movements now. We upload pictures and films to the Internet. The beta-versions of programs that analyze these files are ready to go. Our values, needs, preferences and price elasticities can be analyzed by marketers. Much user and transaction data lies scattered around a number of databases. The 'only' thing missing is the intelligent linking and use of them, which is 'only' a question of time, intelligence and computing power. The thought experiment aims to show that we can improve marketing in line with data protection – and a right to privacy

– without buying into an Orwellian nightmare. So what would we know in this scenario of a transparent market? In short, we would know who is buying what and for what reason. We could quantify exactly the individual's customer value. We would know which behavioural drivers are of paramount importance for each individual's purchasing decisions. We would know who has which priorities for which products for what reason when they go shopping, and which products can be substituted by other products. Even in the unstable, always highly contextually dependent category of price sensitivity, we would be able to predict fairly accurately at the level of the individual customer what their pain threshold is and where producers throw away margins because their prices are too low or where discounts for price decisions are unnecessary.

The best street map would have a 1:1 scale, but it would unfortunately not fit into the glove compartment! The situation is similar regarding the view of the customer. In most cases we do not need a mosaic of the market in HD definition where we can recognize each pixel individually and turn it around three times.

The question of how precise the mosaic of the market can, must or should be is one that the customer himself decides in the end through his demand for and acceptance of the products tailored to him. In order to improve marketing by leaps and bounds, today a mosaic of the market with the granularity of Bisazza tiles is sufficient: i.e. of the size of those roughly 2 cm by 2 cm tiles that we know from 1950s bathrooms and which are currently experiencing a renaissance. For Bisazza-level marketing, we do not need any marketing Big Brother.

Behavioural Drivers and Behaviour

What do we know today about the steps in the customer's head that lead to a contract being signed? Two kinds of data are of relevance:

data about behavioural drivers and data about the customer's actual behaviour.

• Companies who use segmentation intelligently and consistently will know the behavioural drivers of their potential customers fairly well. They result from demographic, socio-economic, psychographic or values data, data about needs (needs which are separable into 'necessary' and 'desired')

This data allows us to analyze segments on the level of the individual customer, at least when the person allows it. Anonymized data about behavioural drivers already allow us to segment relatively well. We can use this to derive conclusions about the segment logic and correlations. For example, a woman in her late twenties in Richmond, Surrey, who works in Communications and has a yearly income of £60,000 has probably thought at least once about buying herself a BMW Mini or Fiat Cinquecento. Citroën might do well to suggest to this woman that a DS3 is a real design alternative and probably not yet owned by any of her friends. This is, of course, a very simple example of targeted marketing on the level of the individual customer according to segment logic. Our day-to-day experience as consultants has shown us that surprisingly few companies have really engaged intensively with the behavioural drivers in segments. Even though most of that data is easily and inexpensively available, completely in accordance with data protection. In brief, even with existing segmentation tools, real turnover potential can be gained, because the competition either does not use it at all or at least not sufficiently.

However, in order to communicate to specific target groups and to optimize customer value at a whole new level, companies must finally move to a systematic observation of customer behaviour. Or to put that more directly, we have to research behaviour in more detail. Like the analysis of behavioural drivers in segments, this is not black magic. Companies simply need to analyze customer interactions along the customer journey. Most companies do not realize that almost all the relevant data is normally already present in their IT systems.

360-degree segmentation: which data is relevant?

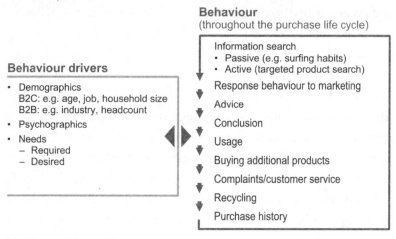

The better and more intelligent we become at linking data about behavioural drivers with data about behaviour, the more finely granulated our mosaic of the market becomes. Unfortunately, most organizations have not adapted to this yet (and the consultancy industry is no exception, by the way). Marketers know about market research and are good profilers, or they are masters at using customer databases, or they have learned their trade in online marketing. This means they can analyze customer behaviour. It is simply a matter of linking up competences. Only then can marketing and sales teams act with a complete understanding of customer value, predict shopping behaviour much more accurately and draw the right conclusions about their marketing mix.

During a project we undertook for one of the world's largest IT companies, we came across relatively refined segments (probably developed at considerable cost), such as 'overwhelmed workers' or 'printing enthusiasts'. We assume the segments were defined and described using impeccable statistical methods on the basis of behavioural drivers. Excellent advertising messages can be derived from them. These messages address values and needs in differentiated ways. In all, there was only one critical disadvantage: no one at the point of sale was in a position to recognize the customers in question and address them with the corresponding messages. So we introduced an integrated segmentation that included behavioural drivers and transactional behavioural data. The result is that now, based on customers' shopping behaviour, we are in a position to match customers 95 per cent of the time to the right values and needs, and thus can communicate with them in a differentiated way.

In observing customer behavioural data, we have to take care not to concentrate only on visible, actual behaviour (information, purchase, complaints etc.). On the one hand, often a considerable part of the behaviour is invisible (e.g. the purchase of the competitor's products, complaints to friends and acquaintances). Here, new technologies can help us to recognize all the important behavioural components (search behaviour in the Internet, share of wallet in retail, posts on social media platforms etc.). On the other hand, we have to try to understand latent behaviour (the customer could find information, buy, complain), in order to influence his or her future behaviour. In addition, we need insights into the behavioural drivers that can be either visible (e.g. amount of expenditure, physical proximity to our shops) or invisible (e.g. available income, values, needs, preferences). This is where advanced segmentation based on market research data can help us.

But what benefits us is the combination of all dimensions that allows us to recognize all the relevant factors, in order to use targeted sales and marketing measures to turn latent behaviour into actual behaviour.

Behavioural dimensions

	Latent behaviour	Actual behaviour
Visible	**Visible behavioural drivers** (e.g. registration data such as income, address, turnover)	**Visible behaviour** (e.g. Internet browsing behaviour, purchases)
Invisible	**Invisible behavioural drivers** (e.g. work needs, purchasing intentions)	**Invisible behaviour** (e.g. conversations with other customers, window shopping)

Admittedly, hybridizing complex sets from structured and unstructured data is easier said than done. And to reiterate, our mosaic of the market represents the ideal situation, where we can zoom in with depth of focus while respecting data protection. There are, however, markets where companies are coming relatively close to this ideal with a do-able amount of effort. The market for prefabricated houses is a good example. No one pays a six figure sum without researching the topic thoroughly (except for billionaires, perhaps, and they do not buy prefabs). A young family that is seriously interested in a prefabricated house will today, in all probability, start to use all the relevant media early in their search. At first, this will be the casual wish to find inspiration and then it may become more thorough online research. In this stage of preference building and the search for information, the first steps in online targeting should reach the anonymized Internet users. The computer's location and cookie information can help – see the example of Capital One in Chapter 1.3 – to give a good idea of the demographic and socio-economic context. The ads have to show houses that match the profile: modern designs for the daring, a gabled roof with dormer windows for traditionalists. That is an easy task, but it can significantly raise the chance of the potential customers clicking on the company's website.

The website itself should give registered customers well-placed service offers. For instance, there could be a data-supported search function for a construction location search that gives the average price of the location's area. This would encourage many people who already have the land for their house to register. The possibility of a retrospective price check is something almost no one will be able to resist, since we are talking one of the biggest investments we make in our lives. The majority of potential customers, whether they have registered online or not, will then request informational material or make an appointment to see a show house. At this point, the customer finally loses the cloak of anonymity and the door is opened for marketing on the level of the individual customer.

Nothing against the intuition and experience of a good prefabricated house salesman, but he will substantially raise the number of deals he completes if he is ready for his sales conversation with systematically prepared information on the purchasing decisions of prefab buyers who are the same age, have the same marital status, drive the same class of car and are interested in houses in the same price range. Market research can tell him all of this quite easily. The number of the most important providers in each national market is also relatively limited. The number of product units sold is manageable too. The prices that customers in certain segments are willing to pay can be worked out from the total market volume and the market share using simple formulae. This allows prices to be optimized at the level of the individual customer, particularly if the salesman looks at the value of the plot that the customer would like to put his house on. Most customers are happy to share the size and location of the plot they are seeking. After all, it helps them to receive good advice. Ideally, however, the customer has already shared this information online.

Customer. Value. Potential.

Let us remind ourselves of the goals underlying data-based approaches to market potential:

- **We want to obtain an improved understanding of customer value over the whole customer cycle (customer lifetime value, CLV);**
- **We want to obtain a clearer picture of the whole market.**

Each goal is dependent on the other. If we come to know each individual customer better, then the whole market is opened up to us. And the more quantitative information we have about what is happening in the market, the better we will be able to answer the question of who buys what when. The answers provide the framework for differentiated customer relationship strategies with the underlying aim of profitable growth.

It is recognized that there are various methods of determining customer value and each method has advantages and disadvantages depending on which market it is used in. In the context of data-driven marketing, the customer value becomes an even more valuable asset when seen over the customer life cycle, as Robert C. Blattberg and John Deighton argued 15 years ago. By way of reminder: before the introduction of so-called Customer Lifetime Value (CLV), marketing focused on two central questions. Firstly, how can I attract new customers? Secondly, how can I stop customers from drifting away? The marketing parameter CLV gives marketers the task of finding out which measures put together will allow the company to sell more profitably.

Putting it simply we can use the following formula for customer value:

Maximum customer lifetime value (CLV) – Present value of future gross earnings from a customer

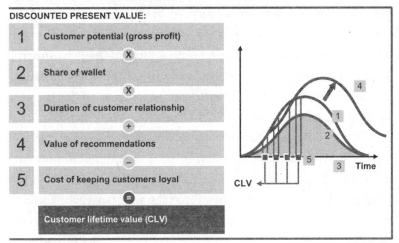

Or to put that in words: customer value is calculated from the discounted cash value, i.e. from the turnover from the customer over the years, minus the costs of customer acquisition and retention, which is also broken down into time series. The potential for up- and cross-selling is part of customer value as well as the customer's ability to bring new customers to the company through mechanisms for recommending to friends (see Chapter 3.2). A number that is becoming more and more important to marketers is the share of the customer's budget that their company has – the so-called 'share of wallet' (SOW). It is equally important to recognize whether customers could, given the right circumstances, re-arrange their budgets for other product or service categories, i.e. the so-called elasticity of substitution.

Marketing focused on customer lifetime value was well received in the academic world from the outset. Practitioners, on the other hand, often had the reasonable objection that the whole calculation works only at a relatively late stage in the customer life cycle, namely once sufficient transaction data is available on a specific customer. By then, most of the customer potential has already been exhausted – or has landed in the competition's lap. Practice has unfortunately shown that the quality of predictions regarding the length of customer relationships and customer-related payments left much to be desired. The predictions were not at all sharp, so the work of harnessing CLV logic and the attempt to market on the level of the individual customer were not worth it in many cases. It was better to go back to the 'watering can' principle of mass marketing with little individualized incentivization.

Various projects have shown us that the ability to make accurate prognoses has become more reliable in recent years. Thanks to the abundance of data in the market mosaic, the CLV-relevant purchasing variables are no longer stabs in the dark – for Blattberg and Deighton, these were still white spots on the map of customer analysis. These variables include share of wallet, the elasticity of substitution and the customer's behaviour regarding recommendations. This in turn means that we have come considerably closer to the actual goal of calculating customer value, i.e. recognizing the potential of individuals or groups of customers for future purchases and using that to optimize the marketing mix.

The bottom line is that a finely granulated mosaic of the market, which includes known behavioural drivers and the necessary amount of data about actual customer behaviour, provides us with a broader, data-supported understanding of customer value. That mosaic allows a company to carry out appropriately targeted up- and cross-selling, to force substitution effects and also gain important insights for their own product innovation.

Costs and Marginal Utility

Data-based targeted marketing increases turnover. Unfortunately, there are also costs associated with customer analysis, the modelling of customer wishes and communication with them using the right means and the right register. We are convinced that data will drive incremental, profitable growth more strongly in the coming years than any other marketing innovation. But of course data-based marketing is still subject to considerations about cost and use. The chart overleaf indicates the parameters that those responsible for decisions regarding the introduction of data-based marketing elements should bear in mind. We are not (yet) in a position to give an exact quantification of the progress of the curve. However, the results of our projects give us clear indications that we are on safe ground when we abstract the mechanism using this model.

The horizontal axis describes the degree of data use. 100 per cent would represent the Orwellian marketing world of our thought experiment. The costs of gathering data and targeting customers would rise exponentially, even ignoring the legal barriers. The vertical axis displays the development of turnover or costs. Every company that starts to use data for marketing can quickly be successful. In almost all markets, there are low-hanging fruit that we can harvest relatively inexpensively. The impact of targeting on turnover is high to begin with, which makes many companies eager for more. The organization's decision-makers need to be aware that

Marginal utility of information acquisition: we do not need to know everything

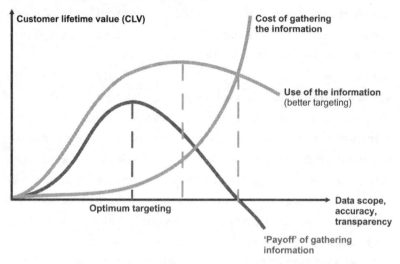

the curve of the impact on turnover will level off or even sink (because of losses in acceptance), while the costs of data acquisition and use will rise with increased granularity. This results in data use for marketing purposes that is counterproductive after a certain point. Targeting's impact on turnover has an anti-proportional relationship to costs.

The challenge for marketers is the same as it ever was: the costs and utility of their measures must be brought into an optimal relationship. And those who understand their instruments will, over time, be able to push the vertex of the turnover curves further and further to the right. What is quite charming about data-based marketing is that, thanks to the abundance of data, we know much more quickly and accurately how much the specific marketing measures will add to turnover. In Chapter 2.3 of this book, we will engage much more intensively with the intelligent testing of data-based marketing methods and the accurate calculation of utility, i.e. the return on marketing investment (ROMI). At this point, we will simply return to the level of the individual customer and to our differentiated understanding of customer value, bearing in mind the chart of the cost-benefit analysis. The critical question is how can we increase CLV, whether of a consumer or a company?

The experience of dozens of projects has shown us that we only have to reach into the 'toolbox' of traditional customer value leverage to find a suitable framework. Five steps lead to success:

1. Identify the market (and so the potential) on the level of the individual customer.
2. Increase the share of wallet of the individual customer:
   a) Sales optimization in the customer's existing product category, i.e. classic up-selling
   b) Ousting of the competition
   c) Substitution of spending on other products or services by providing new innovative offers that correspond better to the customers' needs and supersede the old offer.
3. Customer retention, so increasing the length of customer relationships.
4. Increase customer recommendations (e.g. through word-of-mouth marketing).
5. Lower marketing costs and / or increase ROMI.

These levers are not new and have been known at least since discussion of customer lifetime value appeared in academic publications. However, our experience as consultants shows that there is often a 'slumbering' potential in them: companies that are not able to analyze data are not aware of this. The following chapter will present plenty of examples of brand manufacturers, retailers and B2B suppliers and service providers who have leveraged considerable market potential from the five value levers. In short, the following chapter tells the story of the people who do it well, across a variety of industries, in all kinds of places, in all channels and in the hybrid world of data and bricks-and-mortar retailing. Every company, whether a global market leader or local beauty salon, can become more successful by using data-based marketing. Most companies will have no other option but to take this route: it is only a question of time until the competition achieves commercial advantages through data. In many industries today, it would suffice if a company tailored suitable offers from a good understanding of customer segments. It will not be long, however, until more companies succeed in recognizing hidden customer wishes from behavioural drivers. In other words, they will recognize wishes that customers themselves do not properly know they have yet.

In a Nutshell

■ Markets are the sum of individual customer behaviours. Big Data analysis provides marketing and sales teams with a historic opportunity. If we put data together in a skilful way, we can obtain a picture of the market in HD quality that we can zoom in on.

■ If we come to know each individual customer better, the whole market is opened up to us. And the more quantitative information we have about what is happening in the market, the better we will be able to answer the question of who buys what when. Data-based marketing is an interpretive system. The whole is revealed by the study of individuals. The individual customer in turn is understood better in the context of the overall picture.

■ Data marketing does not need fundamentally new

parameters or metrics. Our classic understanding of customer value and behavioural drivers is largely sufficient for the application of data-driven marketing. This means that sales and marketing departments will not do everything different in future, just much better.

■ A finely granulated mosaic of the market, which includes known behavioural drivers and the necessary amount of data about actual customer behaviour, provides us with a broader, data-supported understanding of customer value. That mosaic allows a company to carry out appropriately targeted up- and cross-selling, to force substitution effects and also gain important insights for their own product innovation.

■ Researching consumer behaviour is not black magic. Companies simply need to analyze customer interactions along the customer journey. Most companies do not realize that almost all the relevant data are normally already present in the IT systems.

■ The challenge for marketers is the same as it ever was: their measures' costs and utility must be brought into an optimal relationship. See the chart on p.82: And those who understand their instruments will, over time, be able to push the vertex of the turnover curves further and further to the right. What is quite charming about data-based marketing is that thanks to the abundance of data, we know much more quickly and accurately how much the specific marketing measures will add to turnover.

■ Five steps relating to the elements of customer value lead to success:

  ■ Identify the market (and so the potential) on the level of the individual customer

- Increase the share of wallet of the individual customer
- Customer retention, so increasing the length of customer relationships
- Increase customer recommendations (e.g. through word-of-mouth marketing)
- Lower marketing costs and/or increase ROMI

What Would Wal-Mart Do? Use Customer Data Intelligently to Grow Profitably

'Risk comes from not knowing what you're doing.'

Warren Buffett

For a good while now, the revolution in customer data has been clear for all to see. Early adopters show that data-driven marketing in B2C and B2B (markets in both direct and indirect sales) functions in a superior way. The list of best practices grows ever longer. The following pages tell the story of those companies who do it well.

Direct B2C – Making Mass Markets Transparent
Retail is detail: Whoever has the data knows the details

The 2004 hurricane season in Florida was rough. 'Ivan' was one of the particularly nasty ones that raced from the Caribbean towards the US coast that year. The big retailers noticed it too. From the point of view of data-based sales, they spotted an interesting correlation.

The weather report is a forerunner of the Big Data revolution. The increasingly intelligent analysis of a growing mass of weather-related data leads to more precise storm warnings. Wal-Mart has continued to refine its data mining methods since the beer and nappies scenario. Then, they correlated customer till receipts and weather data. Now, common sense will tell you that people who guess they might temporarily lose electricity, and perhaps tap water, will probably stock up on gallons of water and on long-lasting foodstuffs with which they can prepare meals easily. Supermarkets with relatively flexible logistics will naturally ensure they have high stocks of (for example) water, long-life milk and cereal. Wal-Mart, however, knows that when there are hurricane warnings, strawberry Pop-Tarts become a bestselling item. Pop-Tarts are individually packed and need neither to be kept cool nor prepared. They also contain plenty of calories.

The fact that US consumers in crisis situations turn to sweet comfort food they remember from childhood, a little like Marcel Proust with his madeleines, is of course logical, self-explanatory and expected consumer behaviour – *once you think of it*. However, even the use of a very large panel in a consumer survey would not find this correlation. Wal-Mart, however, sent truckloads of Pop-Tarts out in time to reach the supermarkets that lay in Ivan's path.[1]

Getting to know the individual customer better and better; predicting demand via 'predictive modelling' that uses internal and external data; optimizing logistics, range and price with the use of the acquired data. This is the triumvirate which turns a retailer into what Tom Davenport calls an 'analytical competitor': a market player who builds his strategy and growth on the intensive use of data. Davenport is a professor of information technology and management at Babson College, a small but elite business university in Massachusetts. His book *Competing on Analytics*[2] put the issue of data-driven business decisions in the minds of many

---

1 cf. Ayres. *Super Crunchers*, p.30.
2 cf. Davenport, Thomas, and Jeanne G. Harris. *Competing on Analytics: The New Science of Winning*. Boston: Harvard Business School Press, 2007.

American board members. The ideas are accelerated by the new horizons of mobile Internet.

Let's now look further into the future of retail. One of the most ambitious field trials at the interface of customer data analysis and the smartphone revolution is being undertaken at the time of writing by Groupe Casino and SAP in French supermarkets. The initiative is called 'Apollo', hardly a modest name from the perspective of the history of technology. The Apollo mission in this case is to use a smartphone app to land products in the shopping trolley in such a way that producer, retailer and consumer all benefit. When the regular customer enters the supermarket, he actively identifies himself (with a loyalty card) at a card reader. From this moment on, the customer's pocket computer supports him with 'predictive analytics' to choose products and give him suggestions, based on his purchasing history, characteristics of his segment and his exact location in the shop. So a customer might find that an immediately usable discount voucher for a particular shampoo appears on his display when he turns into the aisle for bodycare products.

The capture of data for payment also occurs right at the shelf as the customer scans the product himself. That has a further advantage: Apollo can recommend a strong cheese that is on offer as soon as a tannic wine lands in the shopping trolley. 'Even we were a little surprised at the efficiency of the cross-selling,' admits Stefan Gruler, SAP's Global Head of Trade Industries. He then names a figure that removes any last doubts that the app might just be a gadget for geeks. 'In the test supermarkets, the revenue per customer rose by more than 10 per cent.' From the retailer's point of view, it was also fascinating that they sold much more of their own-brand goods with the app. More of their own brand in the trolley naturally means better profit margins for the retailer. Casino and SAP are now working hard to roll out the localized marketing application across the retailer's shops.

Incidentally, one-to-one targeting for traditional shops does not just have to be on a customer's personal gadget. Screen ads can also be individualized, thus reducing wastage considerably. In Asia, systems are being developed that filter passing customers into categories such as male and female, old and young, and match appropriate advertising messages to them. In Germany, Aral petrol stations have screens built into the dishes where people place their change when they pay. The messages are not yet aimed at individual customers but they are still flexible regarding profitable sales in the petrol station's shop. Individualization on in-store screens will be the next step. We are taking this step right now in a pilot project with a large chain of department stores. Screens will be installed in the customers' line of sight at each set of tills. When the sales assistant puts the loyalty card into the card reader, the analytics start up in the background. If the customer buys three jars of baby food on the ground floor, for example, he will immediately see the message that loyalty card holders are receiving a 10 per cent discount today on everything in the baby section on the fourth floor.

In 1994, Netscape made the Internet compatible with everyone. Since then, the World Wide Web has become a powerful consumer tool, making markets transparent in a way they never were before. The price comparison sites that bricks-and-mortar retailers fear are only the most obvious example. Since Netscape's launch, online retail and service providers have taken substantial market share away from offline business. Mobile Internet means that now, as Mark Weiser phrased it, transparency has become ubiquitous. Interestingly, that might lead to a turning point in the relationship between online and offline retail. As we hinted at in Chapter 1.3, gradually the smartphone is removing the boundaries between the two worlds. High street trade has long had the impression that it is cannibalized by online retail. The customer goes into the shop, is given detailed advice – and then he goes home and buys the same product more cheaply on the Internet. Now experience is showing that offline retail also profits. Customers are inspired to buy something on the Internet by, for example, a Facebook post about a fashion item that they read on the bus on their way to the city centre. At the end of their journey, they go into a shop that they searched for online and buy the item.

Customers – whether the end consumer or companies – have come to know and appreciate the strengths of all sales channels. They will continue to use all available channels and make a contextual decision according to the four marketing Ps. In the coming years, the real battle for the B2C and B2B buyers will not be along a high street v. Internet divide. In the era of ubiquitous computing intelligence and an economy based on cloud comput-ing, the marketing mantra will be 'to use customer data wherever it is'.

Even the smallest corner shops can do that. Or at least they can in the United States. A little white box with an audio jack and a slit for swiping credit cards is causing a sensation. The box is called 'Square'. It was invented by the Twitter co-founder Jack Dorsey. Square turns an iPhone or Android phone into a credit card termi-nal for every small business. The retailer just connects the Square via the audio jack to the phone and he is ready to accept cards. The gadget itself does not cost anything. Square earns 2.75 per cent of the transaction price. The customer signs for it on the screen of his phone.

The most striking aspect of this app is that in the background it delivers business analytics for the small business. One of the authors' friends, living in San Francisco, was surprised when his knife sharpener reminded him on his third visit that the big set of Japanese knives he had brought to him on his first visit probably needed to be sharpened again. Back home in his kitchen, he discovered the man was right. He was back in the shop the following week.

In South Korea, Tesco Homeplus has created a cutting-edge store at the interface of the physical world, online retail and mobile Internet. It is on the wall – literally. In the Seoul metro system, giant posters show a range of products at their actual size. Commuters on the way to work scan the quickly revolving products' QR codes with their smartphones. In the evening, a deliveryman brings the products to their homes. The first figures suggest the pilot project is a success. In just a few weeks, 10,000 people tried out the mobile and virtual shopping experience and Tesco's South Korean online sales went up by a tidy 130 per cent.[3]

Metro is testing smartphone apps that are technologically equally advanced in their real 'Future Store'. Like the micro-sites from Best Buy, they can provide customers with additional information about products, as well as helping them with individual dietary plans and keeping a digital shopping list based on previous purchases. Purchases can be paid for with a fingerprint at the till.

We are curious to know which of these applications will change the future of retail and how. Here and now, the Dodenhof company proves that a retailer need not be a big player in order to use customer data profitably. The North German family company uses the power

---

3 'Shoppen im Untergrund' ('Shopping Underground'), *Technology Review*, 6 July 2011.

of data on a plain 20 miles from the city of Bremen. In the small village of Posthausen, Dodenhof has built a large shopping centre over the years. It has 20,000 square metres of fashion shops, 40,000 square metres of furniture and homeware, 9,000 square metres of department stores, 10,000 square metres of sports and technology stores as well as a 3,500 square metre supermarket. The range is complemented by a home improvements store and a shop for child-renswear. All the shops give out loyalty cards with a discount scheme. As the cards say, 'The good card for good friends'. That might look quite basic and not particularly attractive to high-flying advertisers, but the machine behind the Dodenhof card works well.

The card delivers 450,000 customers' data to the data ware-house. This allows the marketing experts to know accurately which man in his mid-forties likes Pierre Cardin clothing but tends to buy during the sales, and which young hedonist does not care about the price when a gadget is all the rage at school. From the clustered data, Dodenhof derives around 140 mailings each year – some for only 500 people. That might not correspond to the ideal of interaction on the level of the individual customer – which by the way would be technologically possible – yet the current quality of the clustering, which is based on far more than 150 million transactions, shows a good cost–benefit ratio. 'Our mailings have response rates of up to 20 per cent,' says Dodenhof's CEO and marketing director Frank Sperl. Averaged across all the mailings, 8 per cent of them lead directly to purchases. That means that the company's consistent use of bread-and-butter data mining meth-ods gives it a response rate that beats the industry average by a factor of eight.[4]

---

4 'Traumhafte Quoten' ('Quotas to die for'), *Der Handel*, issue 7–8, 2010.

The Dodenhof case shows that the old marketing truth that 'every business is local' gains a new dimension in relation to customer value. Yes, a data net is spread over the physical world now and the highly gifted quantitative analysts, often called 'quants' for short, can find connections in these global data sets that create added value. However, clever businesses can achieve quick success in clearly delimited economic units by using tried and tested tools for analyzing customer data.

In many conversations with our customers we note that in the wave of online shop building many companies do not think enough about how to integrate old offline and new online channels right from the start. Admittedly, if you are setting up substantial online channels, you will be busy simply getting your shop up and running with good online marketing, setting up good logistics and a call centre that can give customers good advice and deflect complaints effectively. That is not enough. Unfortunately, there is no way around the fact that if you want to be successful in the future, you will need to create data linkage between all the channels. The earlier this is considered and put into practice in the investment in online shops, the sooner companies will be able to predict customer behaviour and make offers that are forward-looking, i.e. well-timed. The key is the need to take advantage of all available data, combining it with intelligence, as the department store example in the diagram opposite shows.

Data-driven Banking

Many approaches to predictive marketing are already available, although they are rarely used in Europe. When we hybridize transaction data and market research data, we can find out pretty quickly that customers in the 'progressive performer' segment will – with X

Department store chain example: Analysis based on all relevant internal and external data sources

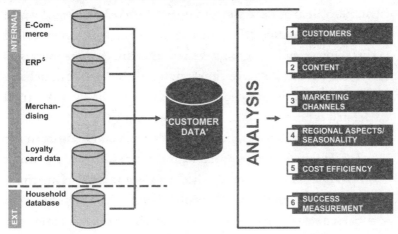

percentage probability – buy themselves a new sofa Y months after buying a home. This correlates Z per cent to the purchase of a new flat-screen television or a freezer. Postal address databases are constantly being updated. Finding out where new houses have been put up is not an insoluble task.

Similarly, banks that sell mortgages and construction loans do not need a crystal ball to predict future demand. All they need to do is look in the customer database. This will tell them the time-frame in which buyers of flats in centrally located old buildings are likely to renovate the bathroom and how much of the mortgage tends to be paid off before buyers of new detached houses in the suburbs put solar panels on the roof. This information is worth its weight in gold to an adviser who works in this area, for example when he has a discussion about the extension of the mortgage. Particularly in

5 ERP = enterprise resource planning

projects with banks and financial service providers, we repeatedly see that there is an inexplicable and yawning gap between the quality of the available data and the quality of their use where they interface with customers.

This impression has been impressed upon us, the three authors, as private customers of large banks. Here are three events that show the customer's point of view:

- One of the authors bought a sofa a few years ago during a move. No discount was possible, but interest-free payment by instalments was offered. All the author was asked to do was send in proof of his salary, in order to show that the customer was definitely not a low earner. However, the paperwork was obviously not read. Because since then, his bank has sent him offers every month for tiny amounts of credit, with which he is encouraged to give himself 'a little treat'. Segmentation result? Fail. Go to the bottom of the class!

- A high street bank contacted another of the authors with an alarmist email. He should immediately, without fail, contact his stock adviser. A certain fund threatened to collapse and there was an 'urgent need for action'. As it turned out, the fund had been downgraded to 'sell' by a ratings agency. Not by the other agencies, however. Over the phone, the adviser was unable to say why the customer had been sent the email as 'this kind of thing happens all the time'. The adviser added that they could think about a re-structuring of the whole portfolio. The adviser should have known that the customer had already optimized his portfolio with another adviser at the same bank in a buy-and-hold strategy and that he wished to avoid active trading. Now, the author knows that banks make their cash from the buying and selling of shares and during the conversation he realized that this was the real reason for the alarmist email. His trust that the bank was advising him in his own interest (rather than the bank's interest) has been considerably eroded. He is now looking seriously at his options to change his stock management and will probably choose an Internet bank.

• Some time ago, the third author bought a house with a mortgage. He and his wife moved in. They have the same address, a joint account and credit card. The bank should also have clear data about their marital status. And yet the bank still managed to shower his wife with mortgage offers *three weeks* after they had moved into their new home.

An unrepresentative study among acquaintances has shown us that almost everyone has a story that shows that his bank neither knows nor understands him. This is astounding: almost no one should know us better than the people we bank with. In many cases, they also have all our credit card transaction details too. They certainly have demographic and socio-economic data. And they have an excellent database to draw on for psychographics and an understanding of consumer values. Even a child knows how important bank secrecy is to us as customers, and the furore caused by the completely legal segmentation activity of a European bank (we will return to the case in Chapter 3.3) shows that the utmost care is needed when banks analyze customer data for marketing purposes. However, in the case of financial service providers the question really cannot be avoided: how do they manage to continually offer me something I absolutely do not want? The three authors of this book would have been content if the three banks in the examples sketched out above had simply glanced quickly at their databases. Of course, there are many banks that leverage customer value in such a way that customers do not mind at all. The German Internet bank ING-DiBa, a subsidiary of the Dutch bank ING, is one of them.

Collaborating with IBM, the Dutch developed a new consolidated foundation for databases. From the data of 85 million customers, every day 4.5 million offers are selected and sent out in a co-ordinated way via all the marketing channels. The degree of personalization? To the individual. Creation and distribution of the marketing can occur in real time as it is based on transactions. The project is relatively young but according to a report by the IT analysts IDC, the bank expects to increase its yearly profit by €20 million. The costs for direct marketing are expected to go down by 35 per cent. The introduction of the technological solution went hand-in-hand with an organizational re-structuring. The traditional marketing silos were removed and a 'Customer Intelligence Team' was created, equipped with the necessary tools to centrally plan multi-channel campaigns and then carry them out.[6]

The Norwegian bank DnB NOR has shown since the second half of the last decade how to do CRM in a bank today. Constructed on Teradata databases, the bank built CRM software with so-called 'event triggers'. For example, if a large inheritance goes into an account, then the responsible customer adviser will automatically be supplied with the appropriate investment suggestions. Generally, these suggestions are based on the customer's behaviour history. The system also tells the adviser which channel, statistically seen, offers the best chance of successful communication with the heir. The tool helped DnB NOR to raise their cross-selling conversion

---

6 Scott Guinn et al.: 'IBM Synchronizes Its Commerce 2.0 Strategy with "Smarter Commerce" Initiative', *IDC Insight*, March 2011.

rate by 40 to 50 per cent. At the same time, the bank halved its marketing costs. And wait for it – doing this gave a measurable increase in customer satisfaction.[7]

Data, Miles & More

As consultants, we fly a lot, and you may be interested to know how airlines use the information in their loyalty programmes. For about 10 years, we have been consulting on some of the most important frequent-flyer programmes. As well as the optimization of routes and load, a central requirement is that loyalty cards can be used to segment flyers according to customer value and to ensure that a higher price in a higher ticket class and the customer's higher loyalty are considered with consistent differentiation at every point of contact. This task is anything but trivial. After all, the same plane is taking all the passengers at the same time from A to B. One passenger sits at the front and another at the back. So what?

Market research data shows that a customer's experience of a flight as more like a private jet trip or a bus journey has little to do with the interior of the Airbus or Boeing. It has everything to do with the whole experience. This is where the advantages of being addressed by name by the cabin crew and shuttled to the plane in a Porsche, which are enjoyed by the few thousand members of the so-called HON-Circle in Lufthansa's Miles & More programme, can make all the difference. This also looks at first sight like a common-sense conclusion. However, common sense cannot tell you whether such costly add-ons are worthwhile for an airline in a very competitive market. Only clean, continual customer value analysis could recognize that a few thousand customers represent 50 per cent of

7 Ericson, Jim. 'Coming to Account', *Business Intelligence Review*, April 2005.

the total profit. And only with the results of such analysis could the multi-million euro investment in optimizing the whole experience of the improved Economy Class right up to the First Class Terminal be justified and more than amortized.

Before loyalty cards were introduced, airlines were scarcely able either to segment their customers cleanly or to determine their customer value. Air travel is a prime example of an industry in which analytic processes have brought substantial competitive advantages to those companies that have seriously tackled the use of customer data. The most important levers are:

- Market analysis on the level of the individual customer with consistent differentiation at all points of contact.
- Increased share of wallet by substantial incentives to fly as much as possible with one airline.
- Increased loyalty and a lower churn rate.
- Increased customer profitability in particular through yield management including targeted price optimization.
- Creation of a platform for continual dialogue with the most important customers, including an active management of recommendations.

As so often with data, US companies took to the wing first. American Airlines was a forerunner. It began to use yield management on a rather rudimentary passenger database in the mid-1980s. But among the blind the one-eyed man is king. Price optimization (followed by higher loads) helped American Airlines to keep the first low-cost airlines in a corner for a time or even push them out of the market, including the apparent rising star in the American sky, People Express, which was clearly out to conquer American Airlines' territory. According to INFORMS analysts, the new yield management system added US$1.4 billion to the company's bottom line in less than three years.[8] Such numbers quickly do the rounds of a well-networked industry, and other airlines got on board. From the mid-1990s, Continental Airlines was one of the companies that set most store by data mining and business intelligence. Continental desperately needed it.

In the wonderfully mean Top Ten lists of talk-show host David Letterman, the following punchline appeared in 1995: 'What are the 10 biggest demands of the baseball players' union? – Number 10: No more team flights with Continental Airlines!' Five million viewers laughed. Everyone knows there is a kernel of truth in a joke. The company's reputation was as low as it could go. The mere mention of the company's name led to a rash of anecdotes about whose suit-case Continental has lost again and which connecting flights had been missed. The business figures were correspondingly dismal.

The new CEO, Gordon Bethune, had the ambition of creating one of the most impressive worst-to-first turnarounds of American business history. His first step was to ensure the punctuality and cleanliness of his planes once more. A simple bonus system for staff did that. They earned an extra $100 a month if the average punctuality improved according to a particular measure. In no time at all, Continental rose from the least to the most punctual US airline. Cleanliness and punctuality are hygiene factors. Every customer expects them, rightly, but in and of themselves they do not provide positive market differentiation. Once the operational housework had been done, Bethune looked for the potential hidden in the customer data sets. He and the CRM team had a few surprises. As

---

8 Davenport, Thomas H., Jeanne G. Harris and Robert Morison. *Analytics at Work: Smarter Decisions, Better Results*. Boston: Harvard Business School Press, 2010, p.152.

with most other airlines, it was taken for granted that the more Air Miles the customer had, the more valuable he was. An analysis of profitability showed, however, that as a percentage Continental earned considerably more from Silver Card programme members.

In spite of a relatively chaotic division of customer data in 45 silos, this finding was supported. And there was a segment of regular late bookers who accepted high ticket prices. They were obviously mainly businessmen and middle management – people with a high demand for flexibility in their timetables. The company optimized the marketing mix to suit those particularly valuable customers and gave them service privileges that only platinum customers had enjoyed until then, such as regular upgrades.

CEO Bethune stumbled on a further (broad) field of data-based optimization with regards to compensation. Here, too, it became clear that it is not the valuable customers who receive generous compensation for cancelled flights or lost luggage, but the unprofitable penny-pinchers who systematically lodge complaints. Closer analysis of the customer data showed that profitable customers rarely complain. However, if they have had three unpleasant experiences they change airline. The grumpy old men with cheap tickets, however, are much less likely to swap airline. And if they do, they are often no great loss or can be won back again through pricing. This led Continental to re-structure its compensation schemes in favour of customers who represented high value.[9] Today, the company has consolidated 10 terabytes from 25 IT systems into a data warehouse from which they can make strategic findings and also take care of customers in real time. The software has an in-built alarm tool that recognizes which valuable customers will miss their

---

9 For a fuller description of the Continental case, see Jeffery (2010), p.144 ff.

connecting flights if incoming flights are late. Trained staff wait for the potentially annoyed customers at the gate and help them look for alternatives or discuss compensation.[10] *Super Crunchers* author Ian Ayres mentions in an interview an airline that installed a kind of early warning system for churn. Algorithms recognize which customers from which segments are unlikely to remain customers for much longer if their booking behaviour changes in certain ways. 'These customers can count on regular upgrades,' explains Ayres and adds smugly, 'At least if they are profitable customers.'

As early as 2007 the start-up Farecast.com showed that flight data 'number crunching' can be a powerful tool for travellers. On Farecast. com's website customers could have the forecasted price development of a flight calculated for them. A classic data mining application was working in the background. It aggregated massive amounts of flight price data with diverse variables including weather predictions and major events. In this way, it could deliver pretty accurate 'predictive modelling'. So the well-informed consumer could beat the airlines at the pricing game by which they hoped to raise their profits with yield management, which we discussed above. Taking a broader perspective, one can certainly see a nice little competition between quantative analysts standing on opposing sides of the counter. It would be interesting to know if airlines then in turn consider the data from Farecast when making their own pricing policies. If so, they would be able to read the market's pricing policy very easily in the Internet. Then the little competition between quants would take on a 'meta' level that changes the playing field completely.

Farecast's number crunchers were winners in any case. Microsoft stepped in and bought the company for an estimated US$100

---

10 Davenport (2010), p.159.

million. Since then, the functionality has been integrated into the Bing search machine, not that it helped Microsoft much in their battle with Google, the best number crunchers of all. After 10 years of data optimization under Gordon Bethune, Continental Airlines rose from last place to first place in the ranking of US airlines and in 2005 received the Gartner Business Intelligence Award open to all industries. Unfortunately this was not enough to protect it from a merger with United Airlines. Intelligence also makes companies attractive.

Jill in the Driver's Seat

Who is Jill? No one at the electronics chain Best Buy would have been able to answer that question until customer data mining turned up an interesting statistic in markets whose catchment area included many families. In suburban America, there is a surprisingly large amount of women who: (often) work, are in charge of their children's education and also make the family's most important electronics purchasing decisions. In short, in many markets a lot of men might hang around in the background, finding out about the newest features of pocket-sized HD digital cameras, but it is their wives who buy. They rush into the shop between office and nursery and as well as a combined fridge-freezer, they look for a new telephone, as the bigger kids want to use their own cordless phone. The Best Buy profilers call this segment 'Jills'. And since they have learned about them, the Best Buy marketers in turn communicate with them by mailings, in-store posters showing mothers, children and electronics targeted at Jills. In selected shops, Jills are even given a 'personal shopper' as they come in, i.e. a well-trained sales assistant who can guide them through the shop. The assistant might not know every product in every section in depth, but Jills have no time to wait for a specialist in one area.

Accompanying analysis of loyalty cards and till receipts shows that the revenue per customer rises dramatically when they are accompanied by a personal shopping assistant. This is particularly true in the case of Jills. More subtle methods are also used to create Jill-friendly ambience in shops they visit frequently. The music there is considerably quieter than in the average shop with its usual mix of customers.

Analogous to the Jill markets, Best Buy has now also tweaked shops for 'Barrys'. Barry is a young male who loves all things audio-visual. If the localized market research detects a sufficient number of Barrys in the catchment area, then the shop is given a large home cinema section. Staff are trained well in products typically bought by Barrys and also encouraged to actively start a conversation about the customer's lifestyle and background, so that they provide good sales advice, bearing in mind the segmentation logic that they have learned. The training goes so far as to teach staff in these shops to systematically research which local particularities result from the demographic and socio-economic data and teaches them how to test their own hypotheses empirically.

Now (once again) common sense would tell you that in every region you will find every kind of buyer of electronic goods and that the segmentation should probably not be overdone. Which is why the new shops formatted according to segment logic naturally had to be tested empirically too. The result? Shops that had been segment-optimized had double the turnover of shops that did not function according to the chain's segmentation model.[11] In case this figure is not convincing enough on its own, let's look at Best

11 For the Best Buy case, see: the Best Buy annual report 2005; 'Best Buy's Giant Gamble' in: *Fortune Magazine*, 3 April 2006; Davenport (2007), p.95f.; Jeffery (2010), p.5.

Buy's main competitor, Circuit City. For the past decade, it stuck to traditional push marketing and price wars. 'Advertise loudly, sell more' – that banal formula is what Circuit City's strategy boiled down to. The company fell into the margin trap and went bankrupt in January 2009.

Cars attract a more emotional response than fridges. In theory it should be the other way round, but we are convinced that car manufacturers can learn a lot from the Best Buy case and from segmented customer communication.

The car industry was one of the first to segment customers and to tailor its own models to various customer segments. Today, car manufacturers make intensive use of market research data such as the New Car Buyer Survey (NCBS) to differentiate themselves from other manufacturers. Again and again, this data shows manufacturers the gaps in the market for certain customer segments that their competitors have not yet thought about. For example, there was the Mini for stylish urbanites, while the Mercedes M class is a good example of a car that opened the way for suburban dads with sublimated desires for freedom to buy sport utility vehicles. The Mazda MX5, also known as the Miata, is a third example. A fun car for fans of sports cars who either cannot afford a BMW Z4 or Porsche Boxster or are unwilling to spend that much on a car. Enough about the success stories. Our projects for car manufacturers show us time and again how wide the gap often is between marketing and sales. Or to put it another way, marketing divisions consider market leadership and segmentation, and ideally this results in a cleverly differentiated range of models that match the manufacturer's target groups. Meanwhile, the salesman in the showroom continues to sell by gut instinct. Let us stress, we have nothing against a good salesman's experience and gut instinct. However, we are convinced that he, like Best Buy's segment trained staff, will sell even better if he knows the segment logic and related regional variations that lie behind the range of models. And if he is trained to profile the customer sitting in front of him.

For what is probably the most expensive purchase in B2C markets after a home, the great opportunity – in spite of Internet options – lies in the fact that the transaction will in all probability only be completed after test drives and long conversations with the individual customer. If the customer shows loyalty to a brand and is thinking about buying another car or a second car, then there will be excellent current data for individual profiling. This is particularly true if there is already a financing agreement in place on a car, for which the customer will have revealed his income or savings. That could lead to the following scenario. A price-conscious 'mid-ager' with two children and a house-hold net income of £40,000 is thinking about replacing his four-year-old Ford Mondeo estate with a new car. He is happy with his current model, but he is also considering changing to a Ford C-Max. If the salesman knows how many Mondeo customers in Europe are currently switching to a Hyundai i40 because of better extras, or to the cheaper Vauxhall Zafira, then he will be able to make better offers than if he does not see beyond the horizons of his own dealership.

Now a fan of intuitive sales might object that there is no detailed data on customer churn available. That is unfortunate, because it would not be difficult to obtain after the event. Almost no car manufacturer undertakes systematic lost order analysis at the level of the individual customer. Yet after having had a test drive that did not lead to a purchase, no doubt most customers would be willing to share the information. You would just need to ask them politely. After all, people like to talk about their new cars. And lost order conversations could express an interest in knowing why the dealer-ship's offer did not convince the customer. This would not only deliver useful insights for the whole organization's salesforce, but also send customers the following message: 'it's a shame it didn't work out this time – but we still value you as a customer.' Car dealers should also bear in mind that the amount of publicly available data about individual customers is growing. With the car trade's high margins and customer lifetime values, it would be worth looking at the social media profiles of valued customers.

No one forces a consumer to make his personal or work life (partially) public on LinkedIn, Xing or Facebook. No salesman should be aggressive in trying to penetrate the private sphere of a customer or potential customer. That would backfire. However, there is a growing number of (young) customers who do not mind at all being linked to their car dealer on LinkedIn or Xing. If the customer then proudly announces on the social network that he has jumped two rungs of the career ladder with his new job, then for the salesman to offer a mutually appealing leasing upgrade cannot do any harm. We know of some sales staff in the insurance and financial services industries who systematically look for status updates in social networks and adjust the way they address customers accordingly. To do that, the salesman does not need to be linked to the customer. The publicly accessible Facebook pages, for example, tend to show when a customer has married or had a child. Or when he has divorced, retired or moved house. Today, there are social media monitoring providers who can undertake large-scale analyses along these lines. Some of them are in India. We will return to social media analysis and sensible partners for it in Chapter 3.2. Regarding the smaller number of regular customers at a single car dealership, it is pertinent to ask whether the salesman could undertake the monitoring himself, when the showroom is quiet? He knows his Jills and Barrys better than an external service provider in India. All he needs is better information about which offers at what time have what chance of converting to a sale.

Churning up the churn

Telecommunications companies have great amounts of customer data, including much that is enriched with demographic information. In addition, they know their customers' usage, allowing them to develop individual offers for them, whether up-selling, such as new mobile Internet services, or to prevent a customer from drifting to the competition. However, there are considerable challenges concerning data usage in the industry.

As is well known, the large telecom companies (or 'telcos') are in a highly competitive market, often with decreasing margins. The IT infrastructure in many telecom companies is highly fragmented. Often there are numerous parallel systems; unlinked data silos form the backbone of the database structure. In every single case this can be explained by the meteoric growth in the industry since the 1990s and by the necessity to continually offer new functionality in an industry that is driven by technology. Today, it is clear that even an industry built on binary code can have large difficulties in handling data.

Seen systematically, there are three paramount challenges:

1. Many companies find it difficult to collect in sensible IT systems all the enormous amounts of data from mobile and landline phones, from mobile Internet usage, technical network analyses and CRM systems.
2. If IT infrastructures are consolidated, there is still a need from a marketing perspective to find sense and purpose in the jumble of data.
3. Competitors from neighbouring industries have developed a clearly superior understanding of customers in the last five to ten years and, armed with this knowledge, they are breaking

into the telecom companies' territory. We are referring to the usual suspects: Google, Apple and eBay.[12]

Many decision-makers in the telecom industry do not have a rosy view of the future. We are afraid that for many of the established players, pessimism is indeed justified. At the same time, the forerunners are using their data in a strategic transformation into customer-centred organizations. They have understood that mobile phone customers demand of their providers a high level of customer understanding, a good technical infrastructure, acceptable service and a fair price. Otherwise they will hang up.

As always with strategically planned and guided transformation, a company needs stamina and the will to take many intermediate steps. In order to get the process up and running quickly, early successes are helpful too, because they send a message internally that we are on the right path; let's keep going. This is, for example, the case in the following three case studies on data-driven optimization.

Case 1: Data-based Optimization of End Device Subsidizing

In almost all European markets, network operators subsidize mobile phones and smartphones in order to retain old customers or win new ones. As surprising as it may sound, this is often done without detailed analysis of customer value and an evaluation of the return on investments that such measures have brought in the past to different customer segments. Yet the necessary data is likely to be available and easy to gather, even if the data is in unlinked silos.

---

12 See also the Roland Berger Study: *What Customers Really Want – A Customer-centric Strategy for Telecom Operators* (2011).

In a project with a large European mobile telephony provider, the Average Revenue per User (ARPU) was linked on the individual customer level to strategic market research data on mobile phone subsidizing. Then we classified subsidized end devices on the basis of the turnover per customer and identified customer groups where negotiation was called for. The realization of the subsidizing policy saved the company at least €10 million in one country in customer acquisition and retention costs. In addition, the analysis helped to improve future mobile phone offers, so that they met customers' wishes better and were more profitable for the provider.

Case 2: Data-based Focus on Sales Offensives

The sales team of a central European mobile network operator spread its marketing budget relatively equally over all the sales regions. Regional market potential was not considered. Working for the company, we aggregated data on the company's shops that was broken down according to postcodes with localized data on mobile phone usage and market saturation. The postcode districts were then divided up into various groups and the marketing and sales activities in less saturated markets were intensified at points of sale. That may sound like a rather simple exercise. It was. However, at that time the competitors had missed out on the opportunity for data-optimized regional marketing. The return on marketing investment rose through a more intelligent allocation of budget.

Case 3: Data-based Customer Retention in Prepaid Markets

A more advanced project from both a technical and an analytic point of view was with a Russian mobile phone operator. The bulk of its turnover and profit came from the sale of prepaid SIM cards. (Russian consumers often use several prepaid SIM cards at the same time.) There is a correspondingly high danger of losing them as customers.

In a project using Teradata database software, the provider defined one early indicator as the appearance of new numbers among the much-dialled numbers of a customer's personal contacts. This meant that the circle of friends or colleagues was choosing a new provider. That naturally also increased the danger that the provider's own customer would drift to the competition. If a data mining application recognizes such a pattern, then the provider automatically and immediately starts its customer retention activities. These activities are particularly time-sensitive, as the provider can only speak to the customer for as long as he still has credit on his prepaid card. Generally, the customer will be sent 'loyalty offers' that match his usage to his phone, backed up by call centre contact. The call centre system was constructed to ensure that staff would always have the individualized offers of each specific customer in front of them in real time. During the conversation, a glance at the screen suffices to see what kind of a customer they are dealing with and what offers are likely to prevent him from walking away.

The conclusion from these case studies is that 'if I understand what a customer wants and does, then I don't need to be the cheapest'. Teradata telecom expert Stefan Schwarz sees technical network optimization as one of the natural opportunities for better customer focus in the mobile telecom market. 'If a customer finds one call a day cuts off, then his churn rate is going to be 100 per cent.' And yet today's network data provide very precise feedback on why a call could not be connected or why it cuts out. If the cause can be recognized, then the majority of the errors can be removed, for example by providing system updates on the phones. The customer need not even know these are happening.

As with banks, telecom companies can take advantage of event-based marketing applications. Because of the amount of data held in call data records and in general customer data, good analytics are needed in the background. A simple example is an automated marketing reaction when the customer changes his pattern of topping up credit on a prepaid card or when the customer starts to phone abroad more frequently.

A more fundamental issue is whether in the medium term providers will support their customers by optimizing charges based on the call detail records. According to Schwarz, around 60 to 80 per cent of mobile phone users in Germany are on suboptimal plans. Providers need to weigh up the loss of margins caused by offering the customer better value for money against the effect of customer retention. Due to the volatility of customer behaviour, in many scenarios it is worth pursuing plan optimization. For example, a customer who goes to France every summer in July will be thrilled to receive in advance by text message or email an offer of an inexpensive package for 100 minutes of calls abroad and one gigabyte of data traffic. If a contract renewal is due that year, further loyalty measures will no doubt be unnecessary.

In industries with high customer retention costs and simultaneously sinking margins, in the long term the companies that will survive are those which shape their marketing so that it is seen as a service by customers. We will throw more light on the idea of marketing as a service in Chapter 3.3. For many telecom providers, absolute customer focus will be the only way, particularly in marketing, to avoid the scenario that pessimists fear of the so-called 'dumb pipe'. This phrase refers to the idea that telecom companies might become simply infrastructure providers while the added value is created for and with customers by smart players in the app economy like Apple (devices), Google (mobile Internet usage) and eBay (mobile payment functions). Admittedly a clear-eyed look at the figures shows that such a path can certainly be profitable for some companies. However, telecom marketers who do not wish to make themselves redundant would be best advised to go down the customer focus route.

Indirect B2C – It's Possible Without Direct Customer Data

Recently we had the opportunity to optimize data-based marketing for a large European hypermarket chain – without directly matching customer data. The biggest data issue for the retail trade is that a customer paying in cash leaves no digital trace. So the first step was to use loyalty cards and till receipt data to identify and cluster attractive segments and previous marketing activity. For the attractive segments, suitable marketing measures were then developed or optimized. These included:

- Flyers and newspaper adverts
- A shift from flyers to online marketing
- Point-of-sale (POS) advertising
- Range optimization
- Television advertising

For flyer optimization, the layout, picture choice, advertised products, pricing and presentation of the prices was varied according to the catchment areas' customer structure. Tests were also made with POS advertising and variations in the range and combination of products. In some markets, no change in the marketing mix was made. These markets provided the control group in the so-called 'do nothing scenario'. (We will return to this procedure in the following chapter.)

The evaluation of sales in relation to the marketing measures in the respective markets proved to be routine data mining. The best markets showed gross profits rise around 2 per cent compared to the control group markets, where neither flyers nor POS promotion nor range was changed. Turnover increased by around 1 per cent. Once the concept phase was completed, a software tool was developed for the client that allowed it to carry out long-term and independent optimization. The tool's most important functionality included the need to process the enormous amounts of data reliably and to measure the success of the respective measures and analyze them in a short time.

Once the system, which we call 'customer-centric retailing', had proved its worth, it was opened up systematically to manufacturers, in order to enable end-customer-related advertising to be created jointly by trade and manufacturers. And that is possible with anonymous data in indirect sales.

B2B Sales – A Quick Glance at Customer Potential

The market targeted by a B2B manufacturer can normally be defined quickly and easily. That is simply because the number of potential clients and distributors is usually at a level that allows them to be easily seen. In the UK, for example, there are about 1.6 million companies with more than 20 employees and many of them are found in easily accessible databases. Depending on the industry, it requires no great effort to obtain an overview of the market structure at the individual customer level. That was proven in our project with a medium-sized paper manufacturer with a European customer base. The core national markets could quickly be prioritized: the United Kingdom, Germany, France and Spain. The publicly accessible company databases were used to filter out, market by market, the potentially interesting customers, i.e. the ones with a clearly recognizable large demand for paper. They were then clustered according to product affinities, such as environmentally friendly paper. At the end of this process, there was a list of around 10,000 addresses and contacts that the paper manufacturer's sales team could work through systematically – with great success. This laid the foundation for long-term growth.

A similar project was undertaken for a large B2B provider in the related fields of plumbing, heating and air-conditioning. There are tens of thousands of tradespeople in each country. After decades of advertising its products to those skilled workers more or less on a mixture of gut instinct and jotted notes, the introduction of a SAP system meant that the salesforce were required to enter certain customer data in a structured way. To be frank, there were a few problems initially. For example, the companies' computers were too old to run the application at an acceptable speed. (The speed issue was quickly resolved with a reasonable investment in new hardware.) More problematic was the fact that the sales staff had about 40 fields to fill in per customer. Even with the fastest multicore processor at work, no one in sales wants to do that.

Only a marketer could presume to ask someone in sales in this industry to fill out 40 fields. Or perhaps an IT provider that wants to sell a big database. Or maybe a consultant, because as a profession we too should ask ourselves whether our love of complex solutions for complex problems is always the right approach. Particularly with regard to data-based marketing, the basic rule holds that if people are to use an IT system, they must understand it. If sales team members feel that there is a poor cost–benefit ratio for their data acquisition and maintenance, then the project is dead. They won't fill out all the fields. Full stop. In which case, there will be no point in sending urgent monthly emails that insist that all 40 fields must please be filled out in order to create a solid basis of data for successful future sales strategies.

In the case of the above project's provider, the number of relevant customer attributes could easily be reduced to a mere handful. Sales staff do not need to learn by heart the codes that designate European industries. They simply needed to divide skilled workers into one of three categories. The simplified data also led to increased data consistency. After a few months, the data sets were then at the point that allowed marketers to draw conclusions about regional deficits and potential. Less was more. The salesforce understood the message and agreed to a programme of double-digit growth based on a comprehensive restructuring of sales.

B2B2C – Better Doctors

At the interface between economic and social benefit, a healthcare company is planning to transform its business model into one based completely on a data-driven system. The company is one of the global market leaders in the treatment of diabetes. It gives away free devices for the testing of blood sugar levels via doctors and earns from the testing. As a researching manufacturer, it has to compete increasingly against cheap competitors, who often sign framework agreements with healthcare systems or providers. However, the free devices are a cost driver, as a considerable number sit around unused in bathroom closets or land in the bin immediately.

The company cannot and will not become embroiled in a price war. The company's strategic aim is to prove that its method fights diabetes better and that this profits patients as overall healthcare costs fall. What is needed is a data-supported segmentation of patients and doctors. The company believes that 'predictive model-ling' will allow it to predict which type of patient sticks to which treatment with what degree of reliability. That is the biggest factor in the system. Because whether diabetes takes a milder or worse course is often strongly dependent on the patient's thorough application of dietary advice and courses of medication.

The manufacturer plans to monitor patients' history of illness, behaviour and the relationship between patient and doctor. The monitoring system aims to help doctors to recognize which patient needs what advice or psychological support in order to contain the chronic disease in an optimal way. Doctors who use the data-based support will then have a much clearer idea of whether a certain treatment has no chance of working with a certain patient because that person, for example, does not have sufficient self-discipline. In the long term, the system aims to help in recognizing which doctors are not suitable for which patients. Doctors who are willing to improve their working methods will be able to draw their own conclusions and become better doctors, driven by data.

B2B in Indirect Sales – Computers and Forklift Trucks

We have been able to see that data-driven marketing can work for indirect B2B sales models thanks to a very large project with one of the world's leading IT manufacturers that we have been working on for a number of years.

The lion's share of this IT business is in the B2B field. In this segment, the data context is difficult, because the products are normally sold via a number of retail steps. Originally our manufacturer knew only about its own sales to the trade. First, we had to develop a channel-based CRM programme – to our knowledge still a unique one – and implement it worldwide. For this programme, the trade gives the manufacturer an insight into anonymized transaction data. That allows the company to know its share of wallet down to one decimal point. This means it knows whether there is realistic potential in the (anonymized) customer for up-selling or substitution. That allows the company and the trade to target marketing and sales resources. The trade carries out the promotion, as it must re-connect the anonymized and the direct customer data.

The qualitative analysis follows the quantitative one. The critical question to ask in this context is what device does the customer use and at what time is it appropriate to recommend an investment decision in new devices that generally will have lower costs? The data sharing might show, for example, that the customer has a high demand but is using aging devices and so there is a danger that the competition's products might be taken on. The system works. In a market that is challenging, because it is threatened with commoditization, the company achieved two-digit percentage growth rates and so also hundreds of millions of euros worth of extra turnover with participating customers.

In a somewhat different but no less successful situation, a large European manufacturer of forklift trucks uses data to add value for itself, the middlemen and the end customers. Traditionally, forklift trucks were capital investments that companies bought individually or in fleets. Since the 1990s, however, the leasing model has become more important. A large European forklift truck operator will already have considerable experience in maintaining and evaluating service data. These costs are naturally a substantial part of the total cost of the machines over their whole life cycle. As with many industrial technological products, forklift truck repairs follow the so-called 'bathtub curve', which shows that there is a high likelihood of breakdown at the start. This decreases steadily. The products work reliably over the main periods of use. After a few years, the service costs rise constantly. Represented in graph form, it looks like the cross-section of a bathtub.

A correlation between sales turnover, leasing business, service data, cost of ownership for the customer and a few further variables allows the manufacturer to represent its business model in a way that is transparent to the customer: in hours of service. This transformation recalls the trend in other product areas that could be summed up with the motto 'we don't want drills, we want holes'. However, it takes the idea of a calculation in terms of performance one step further. The manufacturer can give the customer detailed proof that he the customer will have it better with the costs per hour of service model. On average, he will have newer forklift trucks in his warehouse and his own flexibility will be increased. Another advantage of this model is that the manufacturer will have to do everything to reduce repair times, because the contract will guarantee functioning machines.

Of course, no one will know the actual costs per hour of use better than a manufacturer with a well-fed data warehouse. The manufacturer's real-time data set, which almost no customer will have, also plays into the hands of the manufacturer. The forklift truck producer is continually researching the worldwide prices for forklift trucks on the second-hand market. That allows him to make flexible decisions about when to pull second-hand trucks out of a fleet – for example when the second-hand market is buoyant in a developing country. And the complete data set of sales, leasing, hourly payment plans and second-hand markets will optimize his production capacities and allow him to deal more efficiently with over-production. The manufacturers' most regular customers have now almost all transferred to the leasing plan calculated on an hourly basis. Internal evaluations show a considerable incremental growth in profit, particularly through the optimized utilization of the global second-hand market.

Crunch!

To summarize, sales and marketing team members who give preference to evidence over gut instinct can choose elements from a broad set of analytic applications and combine these applications in a variety of ways. We have used the case studies above to show which data-based tools can be used for classic leveraging of customer life-cycle management.

The message behind all these methods can be given in one word: crunch! If you crunch the data, you will survive in the market. There will be many intermediate steps before an organization becomes one of the most intelligent users of data in its industry. On the way there, the five customer value levers provide useful guidance about where data can contribute to a better understanding of customers. More and more of our customers have decided to become real 'analytical competitors'. They have either completely changed their business model with the help of data, or are working on it now. And they can prove that it is worth it.

Crunch! The most important tools for data-based marketing

Identify customer potential at individual customer level	Raise the share of wallet
• Systematically record the addressable market – Transactional data analysis – User profiles – Customer account data analysis – Data sharing (e.g. with retailers) – Buying data from data brokers – Regional segmentation data	• Systematically optimize the product range by analyzing shopping baskets • Ensure up-selling through 'predictive modelling' of customer needs • Tap into cross-selling potential • Time the campaigns better – right down to daily offers (e.g. based on weather info) • Provide customized real-time offers • Optimize prices at segment and customer level

Increase customer recommendations, optimize interaction
• Systematically manage social networks
• Provide targeted incentives for recommendations

• Better targeting of campaigns • Optimize subsidies per customer / channel / partner • Coordinate the overall value chain better (cost to serve)	• Use systematic customer life-cycle management for event-based customer contact • Systematically customize the marketing mix (product/ service, communications, price and sales channel) • Systematically analyze lost orders • Improve complaints management (proactive and generous handling of problems)
Increase profitability/ROMI	Boost customer loyalty

In a Nutshell

- Analytic market leaders construct strategies and growth based on an intensive use of data. Here are retail trade examples:
  - After its first discoveries with beer and nappies, Wal-Mart has continued to refine its data mining methods – it has even correlated till receipts with weather data. That is why the largest retailer knows that hurricane warnings are accompanied by rocketing sales of strawberry Pop-Tarts.
  - The 'Apollo Project' from Casino and SAP combines the advantages of online and bricks-and-mortar retailing. A smartphone app allows the retailer to communicate intelligent product tips like Amazon and to combine that with vouchers and bundling offers in real time. In test markets, the turnover per customer rose by over 10 per cent. The app had the added advantage for the retailer of increasing the amount of own-brand sales.
- High street trade has long had the impression that it is cannibalized by online retail. The customer goes into the shop, is given detailed advice – and then he or she goes home and buys the same product more cheaply on the Internet. Now experience is showing that offline retail also profits. The customers are inspired to buy something on the Internet, for example by a Facebook post about a fashion item that they read on the bus on their way to the city centre. At the end of their journey, they go into a shop that they found on the Internet. Bricks-and-mortar retail needs to recognize this trend and use it with intelligent online activity.

- Customers have come to know and appreciate the strengths of all sales channels. They will continue to use all available channels and make a contextual decision according to the four marketing Ps. In the coming years the real battle for buyers will not be along a high street v. Internet divide. In the era of ubiquitous computing intelligence and an economy based on cloud computing, the marketing mantra will be 'to use customer data wherever it is'.

- In the continuing wave of online shop building, many companies do not think enough about how to integrate old offline and new online channels right from the start. It is hard work. Unfortunately there is no way around it. Whoever wants to be successful in the future has to link data through all the channels.

- Some companies or sales staff look systematically for status updates in social networks and adjust the way they address customers accordingly. To do that, the salesman does not need to be linked to the customer: the social networks' publicly available contact pages show much valuable information. Social media analysis is a great opportunity for personalized online advertising, but it is even more valuable for business models that involve personal contact with customers.

- B2B producers can normally define the market they address both quickly and down to the individual customer level. For one thing, there are normally manageable numbers of potential customers and middlemen. Secondly, a large proportion of the potential market is captured in easily accessible databases.

- Data-based marketing can work excellently in indirect sales, both in the B2C and B2B markets. In these cases, manufacturer and trade need to co-operate and use their databases and information in a complimentary and targeted way. In addition to technical co-operation, the key to success is mutual trust.
- Crunch! Whoever crunches the data will survive in the market. The traditional levers of customer value act as a good structure to enable data to contribute to a better understanding of the customer.

Test the Test! Successfully Measuring Success

'=rand()'

Random Number Generator Function in Excel

In South Africa, small loans are big business. Especially short-term loans in the region of £100. Seven million South Africans use loans of around this size to pay upcoming bills or to fulfil a consumer wish in the short term. It is comparable to the credit card habits of US consumers. A few years ago, one of the market's largest loan providers ran a large-scale test. Credit Indemnity's marketers sent advertising mail to 50,000 customers. The interest rate was a randomized figure between 3.25 and 11.75 per cent. It will not have surprised either the marketers or the managers of Credit Indemnity that better rates of interest led to more loans being taken out. What was more surprising was that the picture of a laughing woman in the corner of the letter affected the take-up rate among male respondents as much as a 4.5 (!) per cent lower interest rate did. An even more positive effect on the sale of credit contracts was achieved when a commissioned market research company called briefly a week before the mail-out. The customer was simply asked: 'Do you expect to have large expenses in the coming months, such as house repairs, school fees, household goods, celebrations such as weddings, or the repayment of expensive loans?' The data was aggregated from all the tests and new rules were derived for group-specific communication. Why should a bank go without 4.5 per cent of its interest margin if the picture of a pretty woman had the same sales effect?

In this case, the data-based conclusions, including how to improve the layout of the letters, were never used, as Credit Indemnity was taken over by a competitor a short while later that did not think much of the previous management's testing. It returned to push marketing without group-specific targeting. A few advocates of the former management's testing method started working for another company and have since then worked very successfully with this testing method derived from medical research.[1] Seen from a scientific point of view, the bank's test was a randomized controlled trial (RCT). RCT is based on statistical comparisons (regressions) that find correlations in data. Effectively, Credit Indemnity tossed a coin for each test person and had a close look at what happened in each control group. It sounds more complicated than it is.

As so often happens, when we want to understand the present and the future, it helps to look to the past. Sir Ronald Fisher, the father of modern statistics, demanded as early as the 1920s that medicines should prove their effectiveness through tests on randomly chosen subjects before they were approved for general use. The British epidemiologist Sir Austin Bradford Hill brought about a breakthrough in practice when in 1948 he carried out a randomized controlled trial of the first antibiotics to be developed against tuberculosis and then published the results. Later, Hill was the first to prove the connection between smoking and lung cancer.

Randomized controlled trials are perfectly designed to set simple questions and receive simple answers, in order to prove causality. That is what makes the RCT so useful for data-based marketing, as

---

1 cf. Ayres (2008), p.53ff.

more and more people are coming to realize. Critical readers might object at this point that tests with control groups have long been common in market research and the RCT does not represent anything groundbreaking. That is true. Partly. We have paid close attention to randomized trials along the lines of the South African bank because it was never easier to toss a coin for whole groups of consumers than it is at this historic moment on the threshold of the cloud economy. We are convinced that the method (or a number of variants of control group testing) will prove to be one of the most important factors in the success of data-driven marketing. From the current viewpoint, at least three observations suggest as much:

1. Once again, Internet marketers are showing us the way forward. Within just a few years, RCT has become a standard tool in the optimization of website functions and in online marketing.
2. 'Analytical competitors' are communicating the successes of their test-based marketing initiatives more and more openly and they often allow external research projects to have access to them. In the academic world, the methods are discussed ever more intensely and their success is also being proven empirically.
3. There is a continually growing pressure on marketers to express the effectiveness of their marketing budget in figures. RCTs and similar statistically valid ROMI metrics are excellent at convincing controllers and directors of finance that the marketing investment is sensible.

In other words, investigating the '=rand()' function in Excel a little more closely could be worth your while. Business intelligence software from SAS, SPSS, SAP, IBM and other providers can also deal with the randomization of terabytes of customer data. Technically adept penny-pinchers can also use 'R', the open source software for statistical applications. In the academic world it has established itself as the standard. It amazes us how few organizations, in spite of understanding the method and having relatively easy access to the software, actually subject their marketing to systematic tests with control groups. Studies by Mark Jeffery come to the conclusion that only 30 per cent run pilot experiments with control groups.[2] That is roughly what our experience has shown us.

The Great Advertising Effectiveness Swindle

We still come across decision-makers in companies who think that marketing is not an investment but a cost. This means that when decisions about sales and marketing activities need to be made, the key question is whether the expenditure is sensible in that particular case. Once again, experience and gut instinct decide whether it is thumbs up or thumbs down. This attitude will die out in the long term. The nails in its coffin will be every percentage point of the marketing budget where we can prove the ROMI. The more control group tests we run, the higher our quota will be. In a Stanford University case study, Gary Loveman once named three reasons staff could be fired in the American gambling chain Harrah's Entertainment (today Caesars Entertainment, which owns 50 casinos as well as several hotels and golf courses): harassment of women, theft and not having control groups.[3] Mark Jeffery claims that ROMI can be calculated on 'more

---

2 Jeffery (2010), p.33.
3 Chang, V., and J. Pfeffer. 'Gary Loveman and Harrah's Entertainment'. Case OB45, Stanford Graduate School of Business, p.7.

than 50 per cent' of the marketing spend of US companies.[4] We can add that every one of our projects that systematically sets targets for success and checks them has survived every budget cut.

If marketers are honest with themselves, the measurement of the effectiveness of advertising has normally been a bit of a swindle (see Chapter 1.1 also). Normally the effect of the advertising was not related to a purchase but to the audience reach and to whether people liked the campaign or not. It was simply impossible to capture the mechanisms that led from the advertising message to the purchase, as too many variables were at play. For that reason, 'measuring the effectiveness of advertising' had a single function until now: the justification of expenditure, rather than of investment with expected return. In the preceding chapters we have seen that the more data points we collect on our journey to the customer, the more accurately we will be able to predict his behaviour. When we look back at activity, the data points allow us to fill a relatively 'flat' number with much more detail than it has had thus far – the return on marketing investment (ROMI).

ROMI for Everyone

The first attempts at calculating ROMI were made two decades ago by Philip Kotler et al in their classic *Marketing Models*.[5] A lack of data meant that their attempts were never more than an indication of what was to come. A good 10 years later, the consultant Guy Powell popularized the term in his book that was itself titled *Return on Marketing Investment*.[6] As a survey of senior US marketing managers shows, ROMI has now finally become an important number on their side of the Atlantic: 50 per cent

---

4 Jeffery, M. (2010), p.104.
5 Lilien, Gary L., Philip Kotler and K. Sridhar Moorthy. *Marketing Models*. Englewood Cliffs, New Jersey: Prentice Hall, 1992.
6 Powell, Guy R. *Return on Marketing Investment: Demand More From Your Marketing and Sales Investments*. New York: RPI Press, 2003.

of them consider it 'very important'.[7] And it is no coincidence that there are as yet no entries for ROMI on the German, French, Spanish or indeed any other language pages of Wikipedia. Yet it is not just Wikipedia that needs to catch up; there are, of course, understandable reasons why ROMI has not yet been adopted everywhere. The most important one is that the calculation of marketing return is a laborious process. When it works, it is worth all the effort, because it makes marketing a calculable business. The main problem is that with an abundance of influences raining down on a customer, turnover cannot easily be matched to any marketing measure. And yet we are shocked to see how often marketing departments present ROMI as simply the relationship between the total turnover and costs. Such methods cannot measure whether a customer is drinking more mineral water because of a new television ad or because it is a particularly warm summer.

There are online retailers who know almost to the cent how much budget they need to spend on Internet advertising if they are to sell a particular product to a customer who would not otherwise buy it. As they also know the margin on the product, their decision is easy to make. If the marketing investment is smaller than the profit, then they buy the banner. If the relationship is negative, then the product is not advertised. Instead another product with positive ROMI will be.

Advertising effectiveness can be measured if we define key performance indicators (KPIs) and work consistently with control groups from the same segment. The test scenario is quite simple, as you can imagine. We compare the buying behaviour of a target group that is sent advertising messages specific to it with the behaviour of a comparable group that has not been sent the messages.

---

7 Farris, Paul W., Neil T. Bendle, Phillip E. Pfeiffer and David J. Reibstein. *Marketing Metrics: The Definitive Guide to Measuring Marketing Performance.* Harlow: Pearson Education, 2010.

Control groups – The key to measuring true marketing success

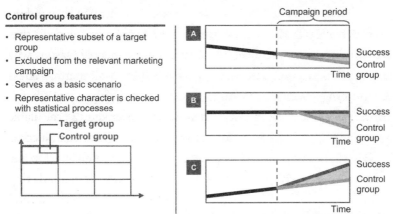

Control group features

- Representative subset of a target group
- Excluded from the relevant marketing campaign
- Serves as a basic scenario
- Representative character is checked with statistical processes

That allows the following key numbers to be calculated.

1. Activation rate: the proportion of the target group that has purchased at least one advertised product.
2. Sales uplift: growth difference as a percentage between the target group and the control group over the set period.
3. Incremental revenue: absolute turnover effects comparing the target and the control group (sales uplift x turnover before the campaign).
4. ROMI: the relationship between incremental revenue (even more accurate would be to use incremental margin) and the total costs of the marketing activity.

The advantage of using control groups is that the effectiveness of marketing activity can be measured in every possible market scenario. In the traditional measurement of marketing effectiveness, the common mistake is that rising turnover – which may have nothing to do with the flyer, radio ad, voucher or personalized advertising letter – is linked to the marketing activity. The decisive question when measuring marketing effectiveness is thus a conditional one: what would have happened if we hadn't done anything? In a shrinking market, a small fall in turnover can be a marketing success. In a boom industry, increased turnover that does not match the industry average might be the sign of ineffective advertising. A valid comparison to the 'do nothing scenario' is naturally only possible when, on the one hand, the control group has the same characteristics as the target group and, on the other hand, it is large enough. Both can be calculated with significance tests. If the control group is too large, turnover potential is lost, which in limited B2B markets is not easy to justify.

Find Out What Is 'Too Much'

Earlier we mentioned one of the companies that is best at measuring the effectiveness of its advertising – a company whose business model is not based on statistics, but luck. Caesars Entertainment Corporation, founded in Reno, Nevada, not only has a US$9 billion turnover, but its clever loyalty card system also allows it to know – pretty accurately – who is gambling in which way at what time. Among the large casino businesses in the US, Caesars is regarded as the champion of analytics. Gary Loveman is not only a humorous man, if you remember the earlier anecdote, but both CEO and President of Caesars and a man who can take a step back. In his foreword to *Competing on Analytics*, he modestly says 'While I hope Harrah's shareholders have some confidence in me, they are far better served to have confidence in the capability of my team to gather and test the best ideas available within and outside Harrah's Entertainment and use only those who lead to sustained superior performance and growth.' Based on the results of a routine marketing test, this new approach involved the company turning its back on the usual packages of enticements for regular customers.

As in other casinos, registered customers of Harrah's (as it still was then) received occasional letters with vouchers worth US$125: this equated to one night in the hotel, two steak meals and casino chips to the value of US$30. A large group of regular users of gambling machines at a casino in Jackson, Mississippi, were instead offered a different incentive package: US$60 dollars worth of chips, no hotel, no steaks. A smaller control group received the old package. The control group's gambling behaviour did not change. The customers with US$60 dollars of chips played considerably more and with higher amounts. The experiment was repeated at other casinos in other regions. The results were the same. The conclusion was obvious: higher turnover and profits for less than half the marketing budget.[8]

Marketing effectiveness was also the focus of a control group test that a large Canadian bank carried out. The bank recognized the market opportunities of cross-selling its equity funds to its private clients. The offer was advertised on television and radio and large posters were hung in every branch. The message was printed on the back of cash machine receipts and put on the recording that customers hear while in a queue for a call centre adviser. In addition, there was an extensive mail campaign. In short, customers could not avoid the information. A control group was used in the mailing. A significant group of particularly promising customers were not included in the advertising offensive, in spite of the marketing manager's wishes. He feared it was not worth 'letting them escape' for the benefit of an academic test. To the surprise of almost everyone, it turned out that the mail campaign had absolutely no effect on the activity's success. The same proportion of customers opened an equity fund account whether they were in the group that had received the mail-out or not. Less would have been just as successful in this case. The mailing was too much communication and so was a waste of

---

8 cf. Jeffery (2010), p.34.

marketing money that could have been well used elsewhere. Further tests will tell us where exactly.

The Campaign As a Business Case

In order to calculate marketing return, you need the KPIs mentioned above, control groups and a little bit of strategic thinking . . . but not rocket science. The key question is simply which part of my market do I want to use data-based marketing on, which part do I want to use campaigns on, and what incremental growth does each advertising pound or dollar bring in? If a marketing activity costs £1 million, brings in £4 million in additional turnover and turnover is the defined target, then the efficiency is 4:1. In most cases, incremental profit is the more important figure. Where the margin is 25 per cent, in this case that would mean an additional profit of £1 million. The ROMI factor related to the incremental profit of each invested marketing pound in this case is $(4 \times 25\% - 1) \div 1 = 0\%$!

The business case for database marketing

Total addressable market
✕ Data coverage
Programme coverage
✕ Reach of campaigns
Campaign coverage
✕ Sales uplift
Incremental turnover
÷ Marketing costs
Programme efficiency
✕ Margin
Return on marketing investment (%)

The example above prompts an interesting question. What happens if the control group develops considerably better than the target group, i.e. where the ROMI is a negative figure (e.g. –200 %)? It can, rarely, happen that marketing does more harm than good. In the case of negative ROMI, however, the first thing to doubt is the significance of the control group. It may, for example, have been too small. Therefore we generally work on the assumption that the maximum damage of a campaign consists of zero increase in incremental turnover and wasted costs. ROMI in that case is (0% – costs) ÷ costs = -100%.

Long-term ROMI calculations are considerably more complicated, as they have to capture more fluid values like brand recognition, long-term loyalty and potential purchases as well as an activity's influence on customer lifetime value, which by definition is a long-term value. Incremental brand recognition can also be a highly interesting figure for companies. This means that long-term and prospective ROMI calculations are gaining popular acceptance as marketing tools in global companies.

Short-term v. long-term success

Burning Money

Yield/Customer

Long-term growth

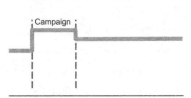

- Short-term increase in sales, e.g. as a result of discounting
- Customer builds up stock and then uses it
- Resumption of normal demand and higher price sensitivity

- Short-term increase in sales that also increases loyalty to the provider
- Long-term increase in turnover

Naturally we do not want to teach a grandmother to suck eggs. Most organizations are aware of the need to measure the effectiveness of marketing. The more marketers who collect information in online campaigns, the more standard the examination of randomized or chosen control groups will become. An understanding of evidence-based methods is now throwing light on other areas of marketing too, whether pricing policy or the choice of certain sales channels. And yet we continue to see that ROMI is much more talked about than actually measured. Perhaps it is helpful to take on board the tip from data mining pioneers, Gordon Linoff and Michael Berry, that every marketing activity should be seen as a business case.[9] In such situations we always compare expectations and results and look for possibilities for improvement.

What hampers the wider acceptance of ROMI calculations in the bricks-and-mortar retail world is that the calculations on their own do not bring added value. ROMI can be increased only when the results are used in a systematic process of calibrating the activities over a longer period. In the fast-paced world of marketing, something else always looks more urgent than the need to consult databases. In addition, somebody three doors down the corridor will always be ready to give extensive reports about how some data mining and testing didn't work. The right answer in learning organizations is that a failed ROMI project will give many pointers to what can be done better next time. Linoff and Berry write down seven questions for their (often technologically oriented readers) to which data-driven marketing tests need to find answers. We have adapted them slightly here:

---

9 Berry, Michael J., and Gordon S. Linoff. *Data Mining Techniques for Marketing, Sales and Customer Relationship Management.* Hoboken, New Jersey: Wiley, 2011, p.22.

1. Has a certain measure reached and acquired profitable customers?
2. Did target-group-specific communication lead to higher response rates?
3. Did the marketing measures retain profitable customers?
4. Which characteristics are true of the most loyal customers?
5. Did new customers buy further products?
6. Which measures / messages worked best?
7. Via which channels have customers reacted to the measures/ campaign?[10]

Whoever can come up with concrete answers to these questions, backed up with figures, is on the right path. This decade's marketing, based on analytic capabilities, is a competitive advantage. Take your colleagues, business partners and customers on this journey with you and you will be successful. That is what the third part of this book is about.

In a Nutshell

- Randomized controlled trials (RCTs) are perfectly designed to set simple questions and receive simple answers, in order to prove causality. This is what makes the RCT so useful for data-based marketing. Online marketers show the way with real-time testing. Control group testing will prove to be one of the most important factors in the success of data-driven marketing.
- Marketing is an investment, not an expenditure. We can calculate the return on investment with increasing

10 Berry and Linoff (2011), p.23.

accuracy. The more control group tests we run, the faster and more accurately we will reach our goal. ROMI is a key number in data-driven organizations.

- US companies today can calculate ROMI for more than half of their marketing budget. The decisive question when measuring marketing effectiveness is thus a conditional one: what would have happened if we'd done nothing? In a shrinking market, a small fall in turnover can be a marketing success. In a boom industry, increased turnover that does not match the industry average might be the sign of ineffective advertising.

- The calculation of marketing return is a laborious process. When it works, it is worth all the effort, because it makes marketing a calculable business. Every one of our projects that systematically sets targets for success and checks them has survived every budget cut.

- ROMI analysis alone does not bring added value. ROMI can only be increased when the results are used in a systematic process of calibrating marketing activities.

- Business intelligence software from SAS, SPSS, SAP, IBM and other providers can also deal with the randomization of terabytes of customer data. Technically adept penny-pinchers can also use 'R', the open source software for statistical applications. In the academic world it has established itself as the standard software.

- Three reasons staff could be fired at Caesars Entertainment: harassment of women, theft and not having control groups.

Part III

Data Makes Markets – The Three Key Requirements

Keeping Customers in Mind – How Data-rich Companies Can Become Customer-focused Organizations

'What scares me about this is that you know more about my customers after three months than I know after 30 years.'

Lord MacLaurin, former CEO of Tesco

Glasses Outside, Too

What does your main target group look like? A few years ago we put this question to hoteliers in Holstein as part of a tourism project. The most common reply was: guests! The North German state of Schleswig-Holstein is a wonderful holiday destination with an attractive landscape, acceptable public transport and some very successful tourist brands such as the island of Sylt. Yet there is real room for improvement in its marketing. In the years 2000–2005, it lost 1 per cent of its turnover annually. The upstart competitor Mecklenburg-Vorpommern saw growth rates of 4 per cent each year in the same period.

One of the main aims of the project was that stakeholders – from politicians to regional marketers and even waiters in restaurants frequented by tourists – would gain a better understanding of who the attractive target groups are for Schleswig-Holstein and how they could communicate with them in a target-group specific way.

In this case, what we find particularly interesting is that the hotel trade is traditionally one where everything revolves around the customer. A good hotel is a highly customer-focused organization.

It knows every customer by name; it knows where they come from, how old they are and whether they are married or not. All of that information is in the registration form. Moreover, there are numerous opportunities to talk to the customer. Service is much better than it used to be and it is commonly recognized that customers are no longer going to accept a product-centric sales mentality in the second decade of the third millennium. 'Paper cups if you are sitting outside' is just not good enough. However, in many respects the industry still has much too vague an idea about 'guests' to recognize market potential systematically and to carry out customer-focused marketing. North German hoteliers, with their blurred picture of their customers, are almost certainly not an exception but the rule.

The first thing we did for the Schleswig-Holstein project was to segment by differentiating the wishes and values of the customers. Our basis was market research data, databases (such as the large German yearly survey Typology of Wishes, from the market researcher IMuK) and our Roland Berger Profiler Tool. The most attractive groups were no longer guests or 'touring cyclists' but demanding connoisseurs, over-50s and families with small children and a medium-to-high income. And what was worth noting was that the customer value of these target customers is higher than that of typical holidaymakers in Mecklenburg-Vorpommern. That was the first important discovery for decision-makers in the tourism industry in Schleswig-Holstein. The alignment of the tourist strategy with the attractive target groups was accompanied by a whole raft of measures. They included a re-adjustment of the grant-giving policy with a focus on entrepreneurial concepts that bought into the newly segmented tourist strategy. The measures encompassed target-group-specific campaigns via target-group-specific channels, an improved booking system and individual projects which reflected the consumption preferences and lifestyles of the three defined target groups.

However, the heart of the project was to establish in a second phase a new, data-based understanding of customers at all levels of the tourism industry. In the ideal situation, at every contact point a tourist will feel that the service provider in Schleswig-Holstein 'knows what makes me tick'. And that he or she will treat me 'as I expect to be treated', whether I am a traveller in my 50s or an affluent mother, for example. In the case of tourism marketing, tens of thousands of people need to have an accurate picture of their customers, everyone from the directors of regional marketing organizations to tourist information staff. The customers have to be at the forefront of people's minds. To make sure they are, on tourism projects we have a rather unconventional method to help people visualize them. We create segment-typical full-size cut-outs, i.e. cardboard customers, each with their own profile including all the usual biographic parameters – and all the relevant information regarding that customer group's lifestyles, attitudes and values. Instead of a vague target group of 'guest' we now have Heide and Gerhard Wellmann from Hamburg-Uhlenhorst: she a retired teacher and he an engineer; available income €3,400 per month; consumer values x; emotional and rational needs y; travel behaviour z. The same information is given out on posters for offices and flyers for hoteliers. Although the life-size cardboard characters of typical holidaymakers might seem like a cheap joke, when used in roadshows for tourism-industry employees, they really work. Three cut-outs out in a row allow everyone to immediately visualize where market potential might lie – and ideally also how they can put the customer at the centre of their activity. Or to use today's marketing-speak (which has proven to be a close relation of consultancy-speak), how they can leverage customer centricity.

The third phase is to combine value- and needs-oriented segmentation with transaction data. Based on their booking behaviour, this allows every individual customer to be matched to their cardboard cut-out with high prognostic accuracy. In turn, this means better communication. Even as heterogeneous an alliance as this one – everyone involved in the tourism industry – can together act in a much more customer-focused way, to the advantage of both customer and provider. That is the point, after all.

Product. Customer. Orientation

Henry Ford developed his Model T in 1908. Memorably, the customer could have the car in any colour he wished – as long as it was black. Over 15 million 'Tin Lizzies' rolled off the conveyor belt between 1908 and 1927. They were the first bite of the cherry for a consumer society hungry to be motorized. The price kept dropping as the numbers sold went up. That in turn increased demand.[1] The cycle of development, product optimization, product-centric marketing and sales stimulus – if necessary, via pricing – had begun. With the next product, the cycle started from the beginning once more. The value creation logic of Fordism worked excellently for almost a century. It supplied the Western world with an excess of mass-market goods and so more or less kept the promise of the more caring version of capitalism: affluence for all! Since the 1960s, and in parallel with the sociological waves of individualization, there has been a phase of product differentiation. Keeping to our metaphor of consumer hunger: it was the age of the seven-course meal. Washer-dryers became standard in homes, MTV brought art

---

1 Friebe, Holm, and Thomas Ramge. *Marke Eigenbau. Der Aufstand der Massen gegen die Massenproduktion* (*Grow Your Own Brand: The Revolt Against Mass Production*). Frankfurt: Campus, 2007, p.13.

and commerce together, children were first given Atari devices and later games consoles. Cars became 'unique'. With thousands of added features in millions of combinations, no premium car is now exactly like any other. However, the basics of Fordist value creation are not really altered, not even in the Nike shop with its individually configurable trainers. Behind the cleverly modular and combinatory mechanism, the automatic manufacture remains at heart a type of mass production.

Globalization gave industrial mass production its second wind. However, at least since Thomas Friedman's *The World Is Flat*[2], we know that the producer organizations in established industrial societies will find it difficult to hold their ground when it comes to mass production. China, India, Vietnam and such countries can make ever more products ever more cheaply. In the short term, consumers in the West profit from good quality T-shirts for £5 and affordable smartphones that can do things that the crew of *Starship Enterprise* could never have dreamed of. The only problem is that all smartphones do more or less the same things and all cars are more or less as good a drive as their competitors. In the globalized world, product innovation can only remain exclusive for a limited amount of time, if at all. That is the real reason why the concept of customer centricity is the phrase on everyone's lips.

The old portion of being focused purely on the product can still be found. Recently, one of the authors was talking to the sales manager of a large aluminium producer. During the conversation, the consultant thought he was travelling back in time to the 1960s – the era when Jaguar still built cars differently and better than the competition and Jaguar dealers would allocate the cars to

---

2 Friedman, Thomas L. *The World Is Flat: A Brief History of the Twenty-first Century.* New York: Farrar, Straus and Giroux, 2005.

customers on their waiting lists. The aluminium sales manager talked about his wide range of successful products. However his last customer survey happened almost 10 years old and there was no precise knowledge about the structure and needs of the company's customers. The company now wanted to take remedial action by updating the survey. We suggested that the opportunity should be taken to develop a differentiated segmentation and so match marketing and sales activity to the needs of the customer groups. This was refused and left for a future date. Too much customer focus at once seemed to not (yet) be necessary here.

There will always be a few industries and companies whose supply matches demand. (Even when the products are much more complex than aluminium.) In the home computer market, there is still a widespread opinion that producers can push their product on to the market come what may. Growth can be planned according to production and sales. The local subsidiaries and retailers are presented with their 'quotas' from 'on high', which are by necessity their sales targets. What percentage is it to be this year? HP and Dell are leading companies in the market because they produce products with an attractive price for the computers' performance and both companies have proven selling skills. HP uses close management of its retailers (which is very good because it is differentiated) while Dell sells direct via the Internet.

Whoever believes a business can be built long-term on the principle of 'more goods, more cheaply' may not need to bother with a deeper understanding of customer value. Push marketers can save themselves the effort of grappling with customer data. However, selling electronics merely by their price and performance is a hard and risky business. The penny-pinchers will arrive when the price is right and leave as soon as another provider from Korea or China undercuts that price. And whoever wants a lifestyle-oriented product buys from Apple. The realization has dawned: almost no one wants to be a 'box mover', because competition with Lenovo and Acer can be deadly. So the key question is this: will customer-centricity become a reality for companies?

A survey revealed that of the 200 marketing decision-makers questioned, over 63 per cent held customer centricity to be an important issue. However, only 42 per cent of those surveyed take customer insights into consideration when making strategic decisions.[3] The difference probably only hints at the tendency to use this term without proper consideration. In fact, the term can be defined quickly and simply as:

the orientation of a company to the needs and behaviours of its customers, rather than internal drivers (such as the quest for short-term profit).

The term 'customer centricity' was trademarked for a programme at the University of Pennsylvania's Wharton School of Business. Trademarking is an easier undertaking than putting the term into practice. A customer-centric organization not only needs to have a corresponding strategy, but also a corresponding culture and philosophy. Under this 'roof', the right tools can be used to build up a comprehensive understanding of the customer, to optimize customer contact points and finally to shape the whole organization as a customer-centric business.

Tesco created one of the most impressive success stories of all on its way to becoming a truly customer-centric organization. The supermarket chain's strategic aim is to win its customers' lifelong loyalty. Former CEO Sir Terry Leahy's marketing mantra was that 'we have to know our customers better than all our competitors do'.

---

3 'Kenne Deine Kunden!' ('Know your customers!'), *Financial Times Deutschland*, 23 October 2010.

Building blocks of a customer-centric organization

The key is Tesco's Clubcard. As we mentioned in Chapter 1.2, many companies' attempts to retain customers with a loyalty card are in vain. In the meantime, the top cards – the ones that have won their place in people's wallets – continue to collect valuable data. When Tesco introduced the Clubcard in 1995, it was a real breakthrough for the chain. The idea had been brought to the company by the consultants Edwina Dunn and Clive Humby. After a short pilot phase, then-chairman Lord MacLaurin said in shock, 'What scares me about this is that you know more about my customers after three months than I know after 30 years.' Since the mid-1990s, the Clubcard's particularly clear system of discounts has been collecting data. For every £1 spent, a point is earned that is worth one penny. For certain offers, the points count double, triple or even quadruple. Customers receive vouchers to the value of their collected points every quarter in the post.

According to its own figures, from its introduction until the end of 2002 Tesco gave out discounts of £1 billion to customers, and every penny counted. Since the retailer started working so closely with data, its turnover and profit have grown considerably faster than the market average. It quickly became the market leader ahead of its arch-rival Sainsbury's. Voucher offers based on an analysis of the individual customer's purchasing pattern and finely granulated segmentation have proved extraordinarily good at stimulating growth. The response rate for the voucher offers varies between 20 and 50 per cent. A better understanding of the customer not only led to additional profits in the 'many hundreds of millions of pounds' (according to Terry Leahy), but also to new areas of business, such as Tesco Personal Finance, which sells insurance among other products.

According to Leahy, without the Clubcard data it would not have been possible to raise the margins in non-food areas as much or to make tesco.com so successful as quickly. The supermarket, which started in 1919 as a market stand in London's East End, has quickly become the biggest online food market in the world. The Clubcard inventors Dunn and Humby are convinced that data smoothed Tesco's path to becoming a fully customer-centric organization. This explains too why Tesco has pulled off the difficult trick of appealing to all kinds of shoppers. The company showed an average growth in the last few years of 11 per cent and is well on the way to taking Carrefour's place as the world's second largest retailer.[4] A customer explained its success

---

4 Humby, Clive, Terry Hunt and Tim Phillips. *Scoring Points: How Tesco Continues to Win Customer Loyalty.* 2nd ed. London: Kogan Page, 2008.

in an online forum in a slightly vulgar but accurate way: 'They know long before I do when my family will run out of toilet paper.'

Since the mid- to late-1990s, every large company in Europe or the US claims that it is a customer-centric organization, or at least on the way to becoming one. The overwhelming majority of the executives in these organizations would be distinctly squeamish if they had to swear on oath in court that this was true. Consistent customer orientation means the 20th-century value creation logic of mass markets has to be turned upside-down. It will come as a surprise to no one if we claim here that data-driven marketing can be the decisive driver of this change.

The Transformation of Value Creation Logic

The buying department decides! Which marketer or salesman in the retail trade has not had his good marketing or sales idea squashed down with this riposte? Not to worry, in future the buying department *won't* decide everything. There was never a more interesting time to work in marketing and sales than now. Marketing and sales have always been the place where the organization meets the customer. In Fordist value creation logic, that interface was nothing special. However, in the era when products and services become almost interchangeable, customer orientation is the last great differentiating factor, moving marketing and sales to the centre of the company. And if these departments do their homework in a timely fashion and – helped by data – develop top-class customer understanding, then they can in fact drive forward that often-invoked and seldom-taken step of the company becoming customer-centric. The completely transformed value creation logic under the motto of customer centricity then looks like this:

Reversing the value chain

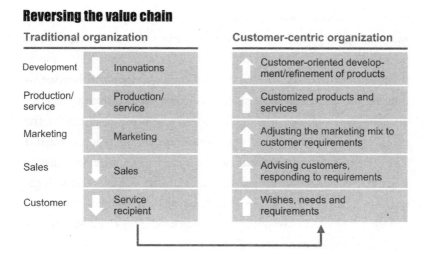

Traditional organization		Customer-centric organization
Development	Innovations	Customer-oriented development/refinement of products
Production/service	Production/service	Customized products and services
Marketing	Marketing	Adjusting the marketing mix to customer requirements
Sales	Sales	Advising customers, responding to requirements
Customer	Service recipient	Wishes, needs and requirements

At the same time, there is a whole series of organizational changes whose end result is to make the people who deal with customers or customer data considerably more important. This includes the higher value placed on communication with customers, new reporting lines in the company, the re-allocation of resources for customer analytics, the integration of lead users and new partnerships with intermediaries to the customers (see Chapter 3.2). It is often most convenient to centralize analytic and planning functions in marketing departments, which in turn allows resources to be made available at each site for direct customer interaction. All of this can be an explosive mix in an organization, which leads us to the deciding factor: overcoming resistance to change.

Organizational change is (almost) always a tough task. This is true as organizations try to orientate towards their customers, too. Even if you might wish for more pleasant causes, crises – particularly ones that threaten the company's survival – are often the starting point to create change for the better. So it is no surprise that after the 2008/2009 crisis, many companies started to look for a new path to their customers via data. We were able to take part in many of these projects and our experience is much the same as in other change management processes. At the start, there is an understanding of the need for new lines of management and goodwill – or at least the appearance of it. In the middle of the changes, trench warfare breaks out and the forces of resistance to change smell their chance. In the worst cases, they block everybody from changing. The old systems work less well than before and the new ones do not work at all. American colleagues have a term for it: 'stuck in the middle'. At this stage, data mining projects often fail due to a lack of follow-through. They do not cause great damage at this point, as the following example shows.

Using the approach described in Chapter 2.1, we were able to report relatively accurately on the potential at the individual customer level for a large European manufacturer of high-tech consumer durables in a B2B market. We could also prove in a quantitative fashion that a data-based change to the marketing mix could bring considerable incremental growth. However, the company's sales teams had been re-structured in the 1980s according to the concept of being 'companies within the company'. Head-office management was convinced of the value of a data-based approach, but it ran into a brick wall when it tried to convince the majority of the long-established local sales directors. The 'companies in the company', on average run by 50- to 60-year-olds, were not to be swayed by any analysis of potential (however clear the conclusions) from the belief that, at least in their personal case, sales were going just fine 'the way we've always sold'. At least in their region they were convinced that all that work with data was not worth it.

Faced with a culture of strong, independent local 'lords', the management had a choice: restructure the sales department completely or bin the data project. They chose the latter. Structures block change. Change managers know that only too well. We could add: structures (often) disable data.

The reputation that precedes consultants is that they draw up (more or less) conclusive strategies, splash them on PowerPoint slides, supply the management with templates for structural changes – and then abscond without any sense of responsibility. We are familiar with the accusation. Consultancy firms need to take the accusation seriously if they see themselves as customer-centric organizations. Admittedly, it is up to the customer to decide whether the consultant accompanies the strategy's implementation. However, that does not absolve consultants of the responsibility to think carefully about and describe in detail the conditions that will allow the suggestions to be put into practice. In other words, how can members of staff be turned into true believers in data-based marketing and customer-centric management methods?

Data As a Catalyst

A few years ago, there were increasing signs that many customers of a large European producer of packaging materials with B2B sales did not feel well looked after. That was not surprising considering that the customers always had to deal with different contact people, depending on which packaging material or which amount they wanted to order. The manufacturer owned a good dozen factories and each had its own sales department. As so often in decentralized organizations, they did not really form a coherent whole. The basic problem had long been known to the management. But only a close and comprehensive look at the databases revealed the extent of the confusion. Customers often ordered at three or more plants at the same time and had to research where they could order which items. If the customer managed to overcome this hurdle, then the sales team only responded to queries. If there ever was sales activity on the individual customer level, then only by chance or because of a personal connection.

At the start of the project, we segmented along classic turnover lines into A, B and C customers. Key account management was introduced at the head office level and all major customers were allocated their own personal contact person. Unfortunately that also meant that attractive customers were taken from some plants, predictably leading to considerable disgruntlement among staff. The re-structuring process was accompanied by intensive workshops where staff not only learned how to use new CRM tools, but where the causes and advantages of the re-structuring were discussed. This process was not abandoned once the new structure was up and running. In follow-up workshops, the team worked out sensible tweaks to the new processes. Crucially, the added value was quantified and discussed in these workshops. The changes' positive effect on turnover, both from the most important customers and in the business as a whole, quickly defused the arguments of even the sharpest critics. At the same time, customer feedback was gathered systematically and here, too, it was quickly apparent that they were gradually becoming more satisfied. In the next phase, methods were worked out and put in place for using data sets to recognize the potential on the individual customer level. In this way, the market could finally be approached in an active and customer-centric way, allowing for growth considerably higher than the industry average in the following years.

Our experience of our own, successful projects shows us conclusively that data-based marketing can be a – if not *the* – decisive factor in the transformation to a customer-centric organization. From this we can derive a series of factors that are critical to success as well as the obstacles to be overcome. Here are five key tips on how to act:

The Route to Customer-centric Organizations

1. Aim for, and communicate, quick success

As described in Chapter 1.2, the simple and effective 80–20 rule is true for data projects, too. Transformation begins with quick success, which increases the desire for more. So advocates of data-driven marketing are well advised to concentrate on the 20 per cent of data that promises the greatest benefits. A clever marketing manager in the US pharmacy and drugstore chain Walgreens had the simple idea of seeing how the postcodes of the chain's 7,000 shops matched up with the advertising budget for local newspapers. These newspapers reach widely scattered readerships, but people tend to go to a pharmacy not further than two miles away from their home when they have a prescription to hand in. This meant the advertising wastage was enormous. Walgreens made the obvious decision: no more inserts for postcode areas that were not within two miles of a shop. The decision had no effect on the figures. The savings to the marketing budget were in the region of US$5 million. The costs for data collection and analysis, carried out on a simple PC, were modest. The ROMI figures quickly did the rounds in the company and became the starting point for further analytic marketing initiatives.[5]

In data marketing projects, easy-to-understand best-practice cases are nearly always the best argument against politically motivated resistance. They offer (middle) management a certain security when faced with sceptics in other departments and superior arguments when dealing with the doubting Thomases in their own team. The results of successful pilot projects should also be shared immediately with decision-makers in departments that could also

---

5 Jeffery (2010), p.29ff.

benefit from better customer understanding (colleagues in development, for example, or in production planning). Everybody with an obvious interest is welcome as an ally. We have already seen in many companies that cross-department networks of data-oriented colleagues become established. Of course, this does no harm to the reputation of the marketing and sales departments internally.

2. Support from top management

It should go without saying that a company's transformation into a data-driven, customer-centric organization is a strategic decision. Generally the change in culture has to be pushed and steered from the top, never mind whatever evidence and successful pilot projects speak in favour of it. In his books, Tom Davenport looks closely at the CVs of CEOs of 'analytical competitors', including Gary Loveman of Caesars Entertainment, Jeff Bezos of Amazon and Richard Fairbank of Capital One. They all come from either a technical or scientific background and are information scientists or economists with a preference for mathematics and statistics.[6] There may well be exceptions, but we have not found them. The intensive use of customer data does not happen from the bottom up. In customer-data-driven organizations, the executives are the drivers of analytic applications. They have to pick up the technical knowledge so that they can ask the right questions and quantify progress with the right metrics. They are present in team meetings and keep motivation up when implementation difficulties arise.

However, if the board or management of a company is not convinced of the power of customer data, they will continue to make decisions based on their 'gut-feel' or conventional wisdom.

---

6 Davenport (2007), p.30 ff.

Let's hope they have some luck to accompany their intuition. This is now a minority attitude, according to a study carried out by the *MIT Sloan Management Review* in collaboration with the IBM Institute for Business Value. Only a quarter of 3,000 surveyed business decision-makers had the impression that a lack of support from executives represented real obstacles to the introduction of data-driven processes.[7] In our experience too, executives complain about the lack of interest in data marketing in their teams rather than the other way round.

3. Gradually building analytic resources – in man and machine
The highly talented 'quants' are unlikely to start flooding out of the investment banks and hedge funds to work in marketing. (The different salary levels in the two sectors should see to that.) However, marketing organizations will increasingly look to hire staff with competencies in mathematical, statistical and scientific analysis. This will be a hard task, considering that these skills are rare resources. But companies do know they need to get the right people on board: two-thirds of marketing decision-makers admit that they do not have people who can interpret complex customer data sets.[8] If recruitment improves, the second step will be for marketing managers to learn to hold on to their analytic marketers by ensuring they are adequately valued in the team. Quantitative analysts often have an introverted personality profile. Conflict comes pre-programmed, as in many marketing departments there is no lack of extroversion and ego. Creative boasters can score many brownie

---

7 Balboni, F. et al. 'Analytics: The New Path to Value. How the Smartest Organizations Are Embedding Analytics to Transform Insights into Action.' *MIT Sloan Management Review* and the IBM Institute for Business Value, Autumn 2010, p.7.
8 Ibid, p.48.

points that prove in the end to be pyrrhic victories. Quants know their worth. They probably will not complain if they are ignored; they will just leave when they become very dissatisfied.

Admittedly, data analysts are not the only challenge for a customer-centric organization's Human Resources department. Companies with a strong social media presence need people who are comfortable in online social networks. Of course, that is not only a question of age, but people in the same age bracket as the authors should not become over-confident about their abilities simply because they look at their BlackBerry or iPhone more than 10 times every hour. Many support-intensive businesses such as Best-Buy, O_2 or Deutsche Telekom are successfully recruiting the 'digital natives' in order to optimize their new and well-received customer service on Twitter.[9] The above-mentioned *Sloan*/IBM study also reveals that the second largest obstacle to the introduction of comprehensive business analytics lies in the capacities present in management. This in turn is a clear wake-up call to boards and CEOs who want to give customers and their data a higher profile in their business processes.

It is difficult to draw up a set of general rules regarding the equipment needed for data-based marketing. On the one hand, quick successes can be achieved with simple Excel or Access solutions. The basic rule, however, is to think about the scalability of new IT infrastructures from the outset. This can require high investment at the start, which might then inhibit a company from embarking on any data-based marketing. So it is worth looking at the scenario from the other perspective too: often the available IT structures, aided by small additional software packages, are sufficient to create

---

9 'Huch, die sprechen mit mir' ('Shh, they're talking to me.'), *brand eins*, May 2011.

considerable added value. In the coming years, this will become less of an issue as the costs of business analytics drop with the evolution of cloud-based solutions. However, the choice of the right tools and partners will continue to be decisive for success. We will look at this again in Chapter 3.2.

4. Data coherence – as a way of allocating work more intelligently in companies

Every individual bit of customer data describes a small slice of reality. The problem regarding complex data sets is that many different interpretations of the business reality can be read into them. The issue of the broad variety of ways to interpret statistics is as old as statistics themselves, and not even in the era of cloud computing is it going to vanish in an instant. We are on safe ground, however, when we say that most of the vagueness and confusion can be avoided relatively easily. For example, we often find that different departments or local subsidiaries use different definitions of customer value when they make decisions or they use different methods of characterizing customers, which leads to different data set formats.

As suggested above, data-driven models of decision-making tend to centralize. It is in the nature of things, because data becomes more valuable when it is centrally connected. Central analytic processes tend to lead to better results than is the case when all the satellites in parallel calculate similar regressions with less analytic competence and without the knowledge of which approaches have already been tried where and with what success. The centralized work can be at a physical location but in the era of cloud computing it need not be. At the same time, the centralization of the analytic processes brings improved data consistency. This does not mean that companies should be secretive about their data. Just the opposite.

Good management of customer data is good knowledge management for the organization. In some parts of the world, particularly in Europe, people have been slow to grasp that information is a resource that gains in value as it is used. If more members of the workforce see the customer data, they will more quickly become mindful of real customer orientation.

Companies such as eBay have experimented successfully in the last few years with so-called 'sandboxes', isolated IT testing environments in which employees can safely 'play around' and experiment with data without being able to do any harm to the main database infrastructure. The best ideas (i.e. those with the measurably best results) are adopted, much like the genetic changes described in the laws of Mendelian inheritance. They can become standard applications for the whole organization. If the data consistency is right and the workforce has a coherent understanding of the company's goals, then data-supported customer-centric companies can overcome the old struggle in management schools between centralization and decentralization. In the customer's best interest, they need to do both.

5. Convince staff: with the carrot – and if necessary the stick
'The "perfect" is the enemy of the "good".' At least that is what people say. Of course, data-based marketing innovations have the advantage that they can be backed up with hard figures. After all, that is partly what they are there for. Yet the introduction of data marketing applications will not free us from the anthropological constant that people tend to overvalue what already exists and to undervalue what is new. We are not going to go into the twin obstacles social and business innovation here – that would be opening a can of worms. What is clear is that the route out of the comfort zone is not an easy one.

When introducing data-based marketing, good change management means using best practices and good communication, as well as changes to recruitment and often structural re-organization, too. The workforce has to be trained to use new software tools and, ideally, be enabled to carry out controlled group trials and predictive modelling themselves. It is useful to set realistic intermediate goals and to keep a close eye on whether they are met or not. Some US companies that are strong users of analytics in marketing have altered their incentive programmes. Results measured against do-nothing scenarios, rather than activity, are rewarded. This bundle of measures will bring most of the workforce round to data marketing. There will, of course, always be a few stubborn people who refuse to co-operate. To deal with them, we recommend Paul Falcone's *101 Tough Conversations to Have with Employees*[10]. Harmony is a sweet poison that paralyzes many companies. Sometimes it does help to use the stick rather than the carrot.

Crisis Resilience and the Moment of Truth

You do not need a crystal ball to predict with a high degree of certainty that the coming years will bring volatile swings in turnover in many markets. At least the uncertainty is certain. Fiscal policy and the aggregated risks in the finance markets will ensure it is so. When change and volatility become systemic, we have to learn how to deal with it. Scenario techniques will largely replace planning tools. Data and predictive modelling will not bring back the secure planning of the 1960s growth markets; however, they will help analytics-driven companies on at least two levels. On the one hand, customer-centric organizations are less affected by swings in the market, thanks to better customer retention than other

---

10 Falcone, Paul. *101 Tough Conversations to Have with Employees*. New York: Amacom, 2009.

companies. On the other hand, analytical competitors are quicker to discover the potential that comes in any crisis. They can model different market scenarios more accurately and calculate results. They can also define the effects of sudden changes to the market faster and react better to them.

In short, the company that knows its customers and develops its business model in line with their needs is resilient in a crisis. And so the circle is closed. Crises are often said to be the trigger for customer-centric re-structuring. Although an increased resilience in crises might seem like a nice side-effect of the process of transformation, in the next few years it could easily become the most valuable asset of a customer-centric organization.

Some companies highlight this development by introducing 'CCOs' into their organization. Chief Customer Officers work to ensure that customers have as positive an experience of the company as possible at their contact points with the company ('moments of truth'). We do not believe that in 10 years' time sales and marketing departments will no longer exist as some neuro-marketers predict. We do think that 'customer experience management' (CEM) will be given a much higher value. Like so many marketing concepts, CEM could be viewed as old wine in new wineskins. Good customer care and communication lead to satisfied customers who are loyal to the brand and, ideally, become enthusiastic ambassadors for it. This logic was behind SAS Scandinavian Airlines boss Jan Carlzon's idea in the 1980s about the airline's 50 million yearly 'moments of truth' that last on average only 15 seconds. These are the moments when an SAS employee communicates with a customer, who then forms a picture of the company. What is new is that data turbo-charges CEM. Data means employees can be prepared when they approach customers and so use the moments of truth systematically to make ambassadors of customers.

In a Nutshell

■ The price falls as the units increase. Low prices increase demand. The value creation logic of Fordism worked excellently for almost a century. It supplied consumers in the Western world with an excess of mass-market goods and so at least in some countries it partially kept the promise of the more caring version of capitalism: affluence for all!

■ The saturation of many markets and the increasing similarity of products mean that 'customer orientation' is now at the centre of many business models. In many areas, service (meaning: meeting customer needs better) makes all the difference to the customer. Consistent customer orientation means the 20th-century value creation logic of mass markets has to be turned upside-down.

■ There was never a more interesting time to work in marketing and sales than now. They have always been the place where the organization meets the customer. In Fordist value creation logic, that interface was nothing special. However, in the era when products and services become almost interchangeable, customer orientation is the last great differentiating factor, moving marketing and sales to the centre of the company.

■ The higher value placed on communication with customers will involve many changes, including new reporting lines in the company, the re-allocation of resources for customer analytics, the integration of lead users and new partnerships with intermediaries to the customers. It is often most convenient to centralize analytic and planning functions in marketing, which in turn allows resources to be made available at each site for direct customer interaction.

- Some companies highlight this development by introducing CCOs into their organization. Chief Customer Officers work to ensure that customers have as positive an experience of the company as possible in the 'moments of truth', i.e. at their contact points with the company.

- A company's transformation into a data-driven, customer-centric organization is a strategic decision. Generally the change in culture has to be pushed and steered from the top. Easy-to-understand best-practice cases are nearly always the best argument against politically motivated opposition. They offer (middle) management security when faced with sceptics in other departments and superiority when dealing with the doubting Thomases in their own team.

- The route out of the comfort zone is long and difficult. When introducing data-based marketing, good change management means using best practices and good communication, as well as changes to recruitment and often structural re-organization, too. The workforce has to be trained to use new software tools and, ideally, be enabled to carry out controlled group trials and predictive modelling themselves.

- There will, of course, always be a few stubborn people who refuse to co-operate. Harmony is a sweet poison that paralyzes many companies. Sometimes it does help to use the stick rather than the carrot.

- Customer Experience Management (CEM) will gain a much higher value. Data turbo-charges CEM. Data means employees can be prepared when they approach customers and so use the moments of truth systematically to make ambassadors of customers.

- Data and predictive modelling will not bring back the secure planning of the 1960s growth markets; however, they will help analytics-driven companies in two ways.
  - Customer-centric organizations are less affected than other companies by swings in the market, thanks to better customer retention.
  - Analytical competitors are quicker to discover the potential that comes in any crisis. In short, the company that knows its customers and develops its business model in line with their needs is resilient in a crisis.

3.2

The New Creatives – The Right Partners in the Data Marketing Cycle

'Ads become information when they're in context.'

Leo Burnett

The Social Burger

Dear Creatives, first here's the good news: you are still needed. The customer data revolution does not make the surprising TV ad, the good claim and good advertising design obsolete. A marketing system based completely on evidence will still need to communicate in the right way, using the right tone and emotionally relevant images. The news that is not going to please all creatives is that their ideas are going to be tested for effectiveness much more systematically in future. Even traditional advertisers will have to throw away their ideas more often, adapt them better and embed them in modular campaigns. And they will have to produce more campaigns more quickly at lower prices as advertising becomes more target-group-specific.

Currently we can see the first big marketing campaigns where agencies with a dialogue or online marketing background have taken the lead. The 'My Burger' campaign from McDonald's Germany in summer 2011 is a good example. The online interaction is a taste of how interaction with customers will often sit in the future at the interface between CRM, social media marketing and open innovation. And how partners' involvement will develop. The campaign started with an open appeal to all McDonald's fans to configure their own favourite burger on an online page that offered 70 ingredients to choose from. Then they were invited to advertise their own burger on their social networks. In the following weeks, around 115,000 recipe ideas came in. The fact that so many customers took part in the playful co-creation of a product was in itself already a marketing success. In the case of the 'social burger', it was just the start of a four-step chain of measurable campaign success:

- Connect. Around 1.5 million voices are heard in social networks. The media value of this is enormous. Through registration on various levels, McDonald's receives wonderfully well-structured CRM data sets. For a large catering chain whose customers on the other side of the counter are usually anonymous, this data is a real bonanza.
- Create. Thanks to the many customer suggestions, statistically valid knowledge is obtained for the company's own product development. A customer playing around with a good online configurator will no doubt provide more accurate information about their wishes than someone replying to classic survey questions along the lines of 'Would you prefer sesame seeds on your Chicken Burger bun or not?'
- Communicate. The inventors of the five successful burgers gave believable testimonials in a TV ad. They were obviously normal people and nice McDonald's customers who really meant it when they said 'I'm lovin' it'.
- Commerce. Great sales made a real success of the campaign. Three of the five chosen burgers became 'mega-sellers' (to use the company's own words). Turnover during the weeks of the campaign rose by a two-digit percentage.

The lead role in the symphony of participating agencies was not one of the large creative agencies but the Berlin digital agency Neue Digitale/Razorfish. In the end, the agency not only programmed the configurator, but also determined the content of the TV and radio ads.

Perhaps such examples are timely wake-up calls for the large creative agencies: they need to get a clearer idea of what they can be and realize that digital marketing does not mean just another channel to be dealt with like the other ones. It is not like a box of laundry powder – same product, new packaging.

The Data Marketing Cycle and Its New Partners

The transformation of advertising and sales in data-driven marketing changes the landscape for marketing providers and the demands made on them:

- There are more partners to involve now.
- The partners all have to be working at the same level regarding concepts and data analysis.
- They have to develop a common understanding of how the new data pools can be used.
- All the partners need to learn what their role is in the new architecture of data-driven marketing. This involves shifts in the hierarchy of service providers.
- Complexity and speed rise.

The cycle of data-based advertising follows old rules: define your goals and create the conditions in which you can achieve them; identify customers; then set your marketing mix; send out your messages, interact and create a dialogue with customers; and finally, measure success and optimize what you offer. The increased complexity of additional channels, the greater speeds, the testing and the evaluation of effectiveness and higher capacity for dialogue all mean that the marketers and sales managers need to steer the process more than they used to. In addition, there is a need for internal partners, such as product developers, to be involved more than they have been historically. They, too, will need to be co-ordinated.

In future, the distribution of tasks between the decision-makers in the company and external partners will vary widely depending on each case. Let's step back a little and look at the data marketing processes with regard to all the involved parties.

Competition raises the game, so from a marketing perspective the abundance of external suppliers is a welcome development. They often have a very precise image of both the customer and the market. We can categorize the providers according to the demands of the various stages in the cycle of data-based marketing:

The new partners for data-based marketing

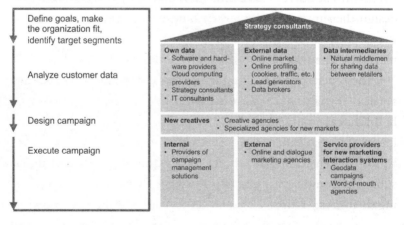

1. Strategy consultants: Define goals and target segments and prepare the organization

Before anything else, self-analysis is needed. What goals do we wish to achieve? Strategy consultancy firms can help to analyze this (and it is naturally in our interest that this happens). The process of coming up with strategy is the core task of the top level of management. If a CEO or management team does not know where the company is coming from and where it is going, then the best data-driven marketing will be of no use.

In future, market researchers will continue to play a part in identifying customers and the addressable market. However, the value of the company's own customer databases and of the customer data shared with partners will become increasingly important. Intelligent and more dynamic customer segmentation will also gain in importance. Marketing departments will need to build their internal competence in this area. Help from outside – for example, strategy consultants – can help in many cases, but organizations that really want to be customer-centric should not let this phase of the process be outsourced completely. In future, few companies will design their own campaigns, but they will certainly want to steer the segmentation more directly as well as individualize the messages. They have to.

If these steps go smoothly, tactical marketing and the sales team are next. If you want to speak to customers individually, you have to build the capability for individual interaction. By now it is common knowledge that outsourced call centres are rarely the best choice. Customer-centric organizations in the coming years will invest substantial amounts of money in feedback channels – not outsourcing their most valuable asset: customer contact.

2. IT service providers: Make the company's own customer database more valuable with cloud computing and innovative analytics

In Chapter 1.2, we saw all the things that can go wrong when customer databases are constructed. The number of decision-makers who with hindsight have the feeling that they should have chosen other technical partners is correspondingly high. The first piece of good news in this regard is that IT providers and IT users have learned from the mistakes of the past. In general, all concerned now think more carefully about what data volume and what functionality is needed for the databases. We are not IT consultants, but from our experience in managing very complex projects we would suggest that 'thinking big and starting small' tends to be the best method of achieving your goals in an IT project. This means that there needs to be a clear idea of what the system should do. The scalability has to be considered right from the start. Then the core functionality needs to be constructed and at each additional step the ROMI of the new CRM possibilities should be measured systematically. Unfortunately, it is (naturally) in the IT consultant's interest to secure as high a budget as possible from the outset, thereby locking in the customer. Someone who has already invested a lot in a project will be likely to invest more rather than admit he or she was throwing money away. So we recommend that on large projects a strategic consultant from another firm is brought in at this stage as a corrective. (Yes, that too is in our interest, but this division of labour has proved beneficial in practice.) Together the IT and strategy consultants can then better help to develop and implement metrics, processes and tools to measure success, thereby also optimizing the marketing activities.

The second piece of good news is that the costs of hardware and software have sunk so much – at least in some areas of business analytics – that certain data mining applications are affordable even for smaller enterprises. Parallel to burgeoning data sets, the last few years have brought a democratization not only of data storage through ever cheaper hard-drive memory, but also of the analytic tools. Not long ago, only large companies could afford the exploratory analysis of large data sets. Today, powerful tools are available for a few thousand pounds; for example, tools built on the basis of so-called online analytical processing (OLAP). Even small enterprises, such as small retailers or restaurants, can obtain standard software without a large investment that allows them to know and serve their target group better. However, in all probability, the purchase of analytics software will be necessary in the future. Of course, the purchase of an analytics solution is normally not the major investment. Without coherent data and suitable processes and all the other preconditions mentioned in Chapter 3.1, the best algorithms are no good. As they say, 'garbage in, garbage out'!

The more cloud computing establishes itself, the more attractive the SaaS-model analytics and business intelligence offers will be. SaaS stands for 'Software as a Service'. Users pay according to usage and so do not need to maintain unnecessary capacity. There will, of course, always be some companies that want to process their customer data exclusively in their own technical structures. Sometimes this makes more sense. However, the trend towards cloud computing will change the data marketing environment too. Crunching proprietary data in the data clouds will not only reduce investment and implementation costs. Along with the increasing use of real-time applications in marketing comes an increase in the necessary computing power (generally by a factor of 10), as well as high fluctuations in the applications' periods of intensive usage. Given such technical requirements, cloud computing will almost certainly provide the best cost-benefit ratio.

A series of technical approaches are also being prepared for the market that compliment the development in cloud computing and that will considerably reduce the classic problems of data consistency that we hinted at in Chapter 1.2. We should stress that we do not recommend that people responsible for CRM should start to say that there is no longer a need to worry about data hygiene. But technical partners like the Palo Alto-based company Datameer are emerging in the IT world. Thanks to their open-source software, Hadoop, they can promise to structure and re-structure data – for example social media data – in almost any quantity according to whatever parameters you wish, in a short time. This process is possible and comparatively inexpensive because Hadoop can link up an almost infinite number of (inexpensive) hard-drives. Datameer's software interface is built like a simple Excel spreadsheet, so that no marketing user needs a computer science degree to obtain meaningful results. The programme can also prepare the results in a graphic form. Another technically interesting approach is to pull the data temporarily from fragmented databases into an separate level and analyze them there with real computing power (so-called in-memory processing). Such tools worked well in projects we ran, for example, with telecom companies' large data sets.

3. Online Giants, Data Sellers, Lead Generators and Cookie Monsters: Acquire new leads with third-party data and see your own customers afresh

Google, Facebook, eBay, Amazon, Zynga and the other large online players collect petabytes of user data and analyze it for target-group-specific marketing. That we all know. Companies by the names of eXelate, c-spatial and Magnetic are less well known. They too deal with customer data, but their business is considerably more discreet. In US blogs, this new kind of web analytics company (of which BlueKai, mentioned in Chapter 1.3, is also one) is often simply called a 'Cookie Monster'. Most of their turnover comes from delivering advertising to potentially interested customers. Previously, this only happened online. You do not need to be a fortune-teller to predict that in the long term they will find other ways to monetize their real-time customer knowledge. The more links there are between the world of bits and the world of goods, for example via smartphones, and the more customer touch points are digitalized, the more valuable this knowledge will be for process optimization and the development of new business models.

One aspect that is as interesting as it is controversial is that data collectors are becoming data buyers and sellers. The legal opportunities vary from country to country, but the trend towards 'data as goods' will not be stopped by restrictive data protection laws. Online marketplaces for targeted advertising are said to have paid several million dollars to the online marketplace eBay in order to use data just from the 'Used Car' category. In addition, BlueKai has set up data alliances with a series of companies that also sit on valuable data riches, including CRM specialists, B2B online platforms and traditional market researchers like Acxiom, Nielsen, Polk and TARGUSinfo. In Europe, similar data alliances are forming right now. This should come as no surprise: the strategy lets the new, real-time distributors poach target-group-specific advertising in the very attractive areas that until now were the territory of media agencies. This also throws up interesting questions regarding the way marketers structure external partnerships. In the foreseeable future, media agencies could fade into the background of media history. Unless they find some advertising super-weapons out of a hat, or themselves start to invest heavily in 'social audience' initiatives (which some in fact do), then they will find themselves squeezed by the Googles and new Cookie Monsters of this world. And speaking of the devil: in summer 2011 the US trade magazine *AdAge* found out that Google is seriously considering selling personalized consumer data, including profiles and addresses. Internally the project has the abbreviation 'DDP'. A Google spokesperson was evasive in response to the report, saying the company was working on various initiatives 'with customers and partners' around the issue of data management[1]. We will be curious to see what data offers arrive on the market in the next few years. The names to watch given by *The Economist* are MediaSift, Gnip and Sysomos. These young companies have set themselves the task of filtering out of the data streams of social media the most economically relevant information. Sysomos finds out for companies in real time what the Twitter-sphere thinks of a product. Customers can subscribe to feeds from Gnip that contain certain web links or key words. MediaSift goes a step further. Marketers can ask which male Twitter user of a certain age from a certain town is likely to be interested in a certain product.[2]

4. Data Intermediaries: New data-sharing models enable effective co-operation in markets

The trend of sharing and selling data is not limited to data and marketing service providers. In B2B markets particularly, sharing (anonymized) data with partners will be extremely attractive. Of course, this is not a completely new idea, but in the wake of the customer data revolution, it will become much more common. Data sharing between business partners along the chain of value

---

1 'Google plant die Super-Datenbank' ('Google plans a "super database".'), *Süddeutsche Zeitung*, 13 July 2011.
2 'Sipping from the fire hose', *The Economist*, 1 October 2011.

creation has traditionally been a hot potato, as it demands a good deal of mutual trust. Retail partners are particularly afraid that the manufacturer might start to approach the end consumer directly – once it knows who that is. In view of the ever-growing proportion of direct sales via the Internet, especially in the US, this concern is not completely unjustified. However, co-operation between manufacturers, wholesalers and retailers brings massive advantages to all.

Transaction data can considerably improve the insight that many manufacturers have into the market, enabling them to optimize their products and services, improve their advice to retail partners, optimize the supply chain, finally put their 'promotional contributions' to the retailers to the most effective use (which is also in the interest of the retail trade) and win and keep market share through target-group-specific marketing. Data sharing can allow wholesalers to offer new services such as 'drop shipping' direct to the customers or packaging of deliveries. This justifies their position in the chain and often raises their meagre margins. Meanwhile the retail trade profits from better CRM benchmarks, targeted support from the manufacturers, lower logistics and warehousing costs, range optimization and comprehensive new knowledge for their own target-group marketing. In this context, e-commerce data can be cross-checked with the manufacturer to receive or trace leads in a targeted manner.

In one project we have guided for years, a major IT industry manufacturer has managed in both B2C and B2B markets to overcome traditional mistrust in the trade. The retailers and manufacturer synchronize their marketing activities to their mutual advantage. Detailed sales analyses in the different segments provide the manufacturer not only with valuable insights for marketing activities in different regions of the world, but also allow it to estimate customer value and share of wallet down to the individual customer level, as well as to optimize channel management, lower his logistical costs and increase potential in co-operation with retail. In order to overcome retailers' scepticism about sharing data, two factors have proved decisive in our experience. The business partner has to have an answer to the retailer's question of 'what's in it for me?' For the IT manufacturer, the answer is contractually guaranteed support in channel marketing, leading in practice to increased turnover, which encourages the retailer to co-operate further on data. The second factor is that the exchange and analysis of non-anonymized data is always via a neutral third party, in order to prevent misuse. In this project, this process has been given the pertinent nickname 'Switzerland'. After initial scepticism and many reservations on the part of the retailer, we are now at the stage where retailers who were previously not involved in the project are actively seeking to join it. Furthermore, participating retailers are suggesting more and more ways to make better use of the data. One example would be the joint optimization of the supply chain with the aim of increasing product availability and lowering the amount of warehoused stock.

5. Creative Creatives: In the world of data-based marketing, creative messages will still be needed – but in a different way

'Creativity' means the ability to make something new. The artistic act in its commercial form has shaped the self-understanding and self-confidence of advertisers for over five decades. The currency for success inside agencies has therefore not been sales figures but Cannes Lions and ADC (Art Directors Club) Awards.

Most marketing managers have always been of the opinion that advertising which sells product is more useful to their company than advertising which wins prizes. However, as long as the measurement of the effectiveness of advertising could not accurately capture the effect of a traditional campaign on turnover, the 'ad award' currency retained some value. In Chapter 2.3 we saw how and why this is about to change. Online advertising creatives have taken on a new role in the last few years in the context of advertisers and advertising agencies. They do not claim that the success or failure of products is solely dependent on their creative genius. Online advertising agencies have always placed the user – and interaction with the user – at the centre of all their plans: it didn't take long on the Internet, which is so much about feedback and interaction, for the principle to establish itself that no measurable response meant no success. In turn, that (often) meant no fee from the advertiser. This also means a considerably stronger modularization of the creative process. In addition to a single inspiring idea, the so-called 'marketing collaterals' are needed by the dozen, i.e. a portfolio of variants for each channel and every target group. Only with a high number of more or less widely varying messages can there be specific communication with the numerous micro-segments. Similarly, only with a high number of cases can data-based marketing's process of testing and optimization work.

An interesting side-effect of the system is that many online agencies have become customer-centric organizations twice over. The end user and his or her device are at the centre of the agencies' communications activity. The company commissioning the advertising is at the centre of their business model. The advertiser has a right to the measurable success of the service and is often able to adapt the campaign itself using drag-and-drop templates. Putting it abstractly, online advertising agencies add input to a continually returning test cycle with an in-built calibration process. Nothing more and nothing less than that. This attitude is making them extremely popular with marketing managers right now.

As a result of the advancing digitization of brand communication, agencies are re-orientating themselves in a number of ways. The classic agencies are still the best at creating brand claims and can conjure up the most emotional images. Yet when creative concepts are required that can be adapted to work for different segments, the most creative creatives have difficulty coming up with the goods. Agencies with a technical background, on the other hand, are masters of one-to-one communication but often lack conceptual originality, precise language and quality graphic design. The struggle for the dominant position in marketing campaigns will be decided where these two fields of competence meet.

6. New data-driven marketing service providers: Completely new forms of customer interaction are arising, for example using geodata

Analytic models are replacing intuition in marketing and sales – but slowly. In the large corporations, this process is supported mainly by large IT systems and is driven by strategic management decisions. As always in technological innovation, lots of small companies are testing all kinds of options at the forefront of analytics – they are possible new partners. Let's look now at three example approaches to help us gain a better understanding of these highly innovative new players and see the spectrum of what is possible in an analytic network today.

Advertisers' intuition will tell them that Franz Beckenbauer is a good face for a Bavarian wheat beer campaign. Yet perhaps Beckenbauer is now getting too old to front a product whose target audience includes groups of young people all across Germany. In the past, gut instinct decided which celebrities spoke for which product, brand or company. The start-up Celebrity Performance aims to take a more scientific approach with its Celebrity

Performance Indices. It matches traditional market research data with comprehensive data sets from web crawlers that, among other tasks, analyze social media posts semantically. Statisticians and mathematicians then have the evidence on which to base answers about the lifestyles of the fans or sympathizers of about 7,000 celebrities. The company's investors now not only include a computer science professor, a psychologist and a marketing consultant, but also the board of a large consumer durables manufacturer.

A MIT spin-off in Boston called Locately is carrying out a groundbreaking new form of market research. It woos consumers with vouchers if they share their mobility profile with them. A smartphone app or the mobile phone provider's data takes care of the technical side. Additional rewards are offered if the consumers fill out questionnaires about their thoughts at the moment they make a purchasing decision.

The Locately analytics tool can see if a female consumer from a particular segment always drives past Family Dollar to shop at Wal-Mart, except for Friday afternoons when she leaves the office early and goes straight to Family Dollar to miss the Friday evening crowds. For its clients, the company combines data from mobility profiles and questionnaires with data from Nielsen and the client's own campaign data. The first level allows marketers to see which customers from which segments drive past their shops. In the Locately analyses, these are categorized as 'missed opportunities'. Regional measurement of advertising effectiveness can also be carried out relatively accurately using this model. For now, Locately does not register directly who buys what product at what place and time. That would, in fact, be the next logical step. As long as there is a clear opt-in policy, it would be neither illegal nor reprehensible. It would really just mean combining Locately technology with the smartphone-based purchasing that SAP and Casino are introducing (see Chapter 2.2). Then the phrase '360-degree view of the customer' will finally live up to its promise.

In our search for new partners, let us finally throw some light on another new prospect: word-of-mouth (WOM) marketing networks. They build consumer communities that test products and sometimes are allowed to share the products. At first glance, that might have little to do with data. The enterprise only becomes highly analytical when the voluntary brand ambassadors have to write down their communication regarding the product. For example, if 5,000 chewing gum testers each speak about the new product to 20 people, whose feedback is documented in online questionnaires, and the testers also write short essays about their experience, which can be semantically analyzed, then analysis is built into the product testing and campaign. Martin Oetting, a partner in trnd, the largest European WOM network, puts it well. 'One of our project managers, who over two months has communicated with thousands of users, often knows more about the product than the whole R & D division of the company. Negative feedback is often more valuable than positive feedback.'

Of course, what to WOM marketers is simply a valuable side product, can also be the start of a separate business model. In the coming years, we will see many new service providers who use customer data to aid in product optimization and improvement. In this field, too, the decisive leap for consumer research is to leave classic survey methods and use large amounts of data to analyze actual behaviour, thereby drawing conclusions about implicit wishes. A promising approach is called 'foresight thinking', practised among other places at the Center for Foresight and Innovation at Stanford University. This method aggregates customer data in the form of consumer biographies and works out which products someone who today is 25 will probably want to have in 10 years' time, when he is 35. In order to work this out, analysts look at the past 10 years' consumer behaviour of 35-year-olds who have the same background and comparable personal consumer values.

Another rapidly expanding field of business will be the clever visualization of data. Good infographics translate statistical findings for non-statistically-minded people. Or as the designer and journalist David McCandless put it: 'Information visualization is information compression.' On his blog informationisbeautiful.net, he collects excellent examples of visualizations that not only make data correlations beautiful, but also more memorable and understandable than Excel tables turned into bar or pie charts.[3] Like this, perhaps even the most creative creatives will find a way into large data sets.

In a Nutshell

- The world of marketing still needs creatives. A marketing system based completely on evidence will still need to communicate the right idea with the right register and emotionally relevant images. The news that is not going to please all creatives is that their ideas are going to be tested for effectiveness much more systematically in future.
- Even traditional advertisers will have to throw away their ideas more often, adapt them better and embed them in modular campaigns. Creative ideas have to be adaptable. Only with a high number of messages can they communicate with the numerous micro-segments. And only with a high number of cases can data-based marketing's process of testing and optimization work.

3 'Infoporn', in *Trend Update*, October 2011.

- Online advertising creatives have taken on a new role in the last few years in the context of advertisers and advertising agencies. They do not claim that the success or failure of products is solely dependent on their creative genius. From the start, online advertising agencies were used to putting customers and interaction with them at the centre of all their plans.
- The increased complexity of additional channels and greater speed, testing and effectiveness measurement, coupled with a great need for dialogue, means that marketers and sales managers will have to give more guidance as they co-operate with external partners.
- As always in technological innovation, lots of small companies are testing all kinds of options at the forefront of analytics – they are possible new partners. They might be specialists at increasing ROMI or useful sources for geodata and social media data or for word-of-mouth marketing campaigns. In future, data-driven service providers will play a greater role in product development too, for example with user-centric approaches such as foresight thinking.
- Self-analysis is the first, crucial step. What goals do we wish to achieve? Strategic consultancy firms can help to analyze this. The process of coming up with strategy remains the core task of the top level of management.
- In future, market researchers will continue to play a part in identifying customers and the addressable market. However, the value of the company's own customer databases and of the customer data shared with partners will become ever more important. Intelligent and more dynamic customer segmentation will become increasingly valuable.

- Customer-centric organizations in the coming years will invest a great deal of money in feedback channels and generally not out-source their most valuable asset: customer contact.
- 'Think big and start small' tends to help IT projects achieve their goals. This means there has to be a clear idea from the outset of what the system should be capable of, and scalability must be considered at this time, too. Next, the core functionality needs to be constructed and at each additional step, the ROMI of the new CRM possibilities should be measured systematically.
- The trend towards cloud computing will also change the data marketing environment. Crunching proprietary data in the cloud will not only reduce investment and implementation costs. Along with the increase in real-time applications in marketing comes an increase in the required computing power (generally by a factor of 10), as well as high fluctuations in the applications' periods of intensive usage. Given such technical requirements, cloud computing will almost certainly provide the best cost–benefit ratio.
- Data collectors are becoming data buyers and sellers. The legal opportunities vary from country to country, but the trend towards 'data as goods' will not be stopped by restrictive data protection laws. The trend of sharing and selling data is not limited to data and marketing service providers. In B2B markets in particular, sharing data with partners will be an extremely attractive option. Of course, this is not a completely new idea, but in the wake of the customer data revolution, it will become much more

common. In order to overcome retailers' scepticism about sharing data, two factors have proved decisive in our experience. The business partner has to have an answer to the retailer's question of 'what's in it for me?' Secondly, the exchange and analysis of (anonymized) data will be via a neutral third party, in order to prevent misuse.

- If a CEO or management team does not know where the company is coming from and where it is going, then the best data-driven marketing will be of no use.

Privacy in the Age of Big Data

'Don't be evil.'

Google's woolly and often questioned motto

Hedonistic Investors

A reliable European bank found out recently how sensitive the media and consumer protection campaigners are to data marketing. Internal papers about a small, harmless and completely legal customer segmentation were leaked to a radio station. The bank had divided customers into 'Keepers', 'Hedonists', 'Adventurers', 'Epicures', 'Performers', 'Tolerant People' and 'Disciplined People'. The internal paper contained some tips for bank advisers on how best to approach customers in each segment. So far, so what? However, the radio station, together with a current affairs magazine, made a small scandal out of it.

In most countries, banks represent a special case with regard to the handling of customer data. Banks know a lot about us. Even if most customers would be unable to give a clear legal definition of what 'bank confidentiality' means, it is a key concept on which customer relationships are built. Banks are supposed to work quietly at increasing our money. Because banks know so much about us, the media, consumer protection organizations, and sometimes customers too, are particularly sensitive. If they get a bad feeling, then they punish banks mercilessly. Perhaps public scepticism about customer data usage will diminish in the coming years but it is true for now that if a bank wants to seize the opportunities of using large data sets for marketing purposes, it has to proceed with utmost transparency.

The first lesson to draw is that customers need to be informed beforehand and possibly even be asked to give their agreement. Secondly, the financial service provider needs to be able to show clearly how their action benefits the customer. Neither had happened in the case of the above bank, so journalists grabbed the opportunity to stir up a fuss. The damage to the bank's reputation was limited in this case, but it could have been avoided completely. We are convinced that a significant proportion of bank customers would accept data mining if a bank communicated that it wished to advise them better and so wants to understand them better. The bank can point out to the customer that insurance product X and investment Y led to high rates of satisfaction among customers with a similar profile. This provides extra data-based information to help the customer make a good decision.

The Company Is Naked

There are – and always will be – a number of industries where the majority of customers do not care what is done with their data. There is little potential for scandal in the way airlines use customer data to optimize pricing and routes, how loyalty cards affect range and advertising, or in the algorithms that an online retailer uses to suggest products to customers. This is all accepted as part of the business because nothing indicates that customers are being hoodwinked by such usage. Hoodwinking customers is never a good idea, but as the pioneering Internet thinker Don Tapscott accurately described 10 years ago, companies in the networked world are increasingly 'naked'. In other words, dishonest intentions come to light more easily.[1] Companies who wish to make a success of data

---

1 Tapscott, Don, and David Ticoll. *The Naked Corporation: How the Age of Transparency Will Revolutionize Business.* New York: Free Press, 2003.

marketing need to be open about their handling of data and communicate its advantages to the customer. That is the moment when marketing will be seen as a service and receive the acceptance for which marketers and salespeople have been hoping for years.

A relatively simple four-field matrix can be derived from these considerations.

The transparency–benefits matrix of data-based marketing

	Low	High
High	**Tolerated advertisers** • Transparent data collection, usage and transmission but few benefits for customers • Traditional opt-ins for data usage for campaigns • Examples: electricity, telephone, newspaper campaigns. • Transparency of data analysis.	**Partners** • Transparent data collection, usage and transmission • Attractive USPs at the same time • Examples: Amazon, eBay, frequent flyer schemes, loyalty cards with discounts
Low	**Unwanted spies** • Little transparency about the data gathered, analysis or transmission • Clear visible customer benefit • Examples: some financial services providers	**Tolerated spies** • Little transparency about the data gathered, analysis or transmission • But attractive USP • E.g. online profiling (including Facebook and Google)

Customer benefit of data analysis

Over the course of this decade, the long-term winners in data-based marketing can only be the companies that create a clearly recognizable added value in a transparent way. Companies such as Amazon and good frequent-flyer programmes manage this. The differentiation helps them to provide better products and services and customers can use common sense to understand or guess what information has led to their being offered which product. The hundreds of service providers who are currently asking customers to allow them to use their data for advertising purposes will find life harder. Whether a home improvements store, bank, power company or mobile network, normally everything is done legally and transparently. If customers know that when they tick this box, they will be sent relatively good advertising – nothing more, nothing worse – then usually no one gets annoyed. Currently, the opt-in rates are still relatively good, but they are dropping continually. The danger exists that in the long term the only people to opt in will be the people who explicitly like advertising. That is about one fifth of the population.[2] If there were more open communication to let consumers know that their data is used to improve products and product selection in the customer's interest, and to optimize opening hours and branch locations, then acceptance would no doubt rise. There is a definite need to improve communication.

It will be interesting to follow developments for the 'tolerated spies'. At the time of writing, Facebook and Google – the two companies with the most attractive 'data for services' offers – fall into this category. Both are regularly in the dock for their hunger for data – including in the US, which is far less sensitive to data issues than Europe. Yet that does not stop billions of people each day from using the companies' web searches, analytics, photo sharing and so on. The overwhelming majority of users share the basic attitude that they do not want their data to be misused and they assume that if such a thing were to happen, it would come to light. But what is on offer has to be paid for somehow and we would rather give our data for marketing purposes than pay membership fees. The long-term success of both companies depends on whether they are perceived to be transparent or to be thieving data monsters.

---

2 *Typologie der Wünsche – 2011* (*Wish-type Profiles – 2011*). Institut für Medien und Konsumentenforschung, p.43.

Marketing As a Service and the New 'Relevant Set'

One of the great opportunities of data-based marketing methods lies in realizing the concept of marketing as a service. Data-based marketing, guided by the right campaign management tools, allows advertising to be perceived as useful. In order for that to happen, the following elements need to be present:

- Relevance. Communicate with the customer only when it is relevant for her.
- Frequency. Do not communicate too often with the customer, even if his or her segment criteria suggest she is suitable for many campaigns.
- Added value. Make the customer an offer that she would not otherwise receive.

Of course, these points should all be obvious and indeed viewed as a duty in 'dialogue' marketing. Yet we all know that this duty is often not met, which accounts for much of the annoyance felt by people contacted in this way. Good data-based marketing will measure, where possible, the level of acceptance in each segment at the individual customer level. In other words, there is a double segmentation. Ideally, the sender knows not only which products or services have relevant content but also where advertising would cross the customer's 'pain' threshold. Or to put it another way: the sender knows the quantity and nature of advertising communication that the customer would see not as a useful service but rather as pestering.

'Marketing as a service' will, if handled well, not only increase the customer's trust in data handling, but in the company as a whole. That remains the over-arching goal. A good example of this is a telecom company that proactively suggests price plans better suited to the customer's phone usage – and ideally not just before the contract is up for renewal. If customers are justified in thinking that the company is actively trying to ensure they on the best possible tariff, they are is unlikely to wade through the jungle of other price plans to find a better option. Analytics that give the customer added value create trust. If we take a wider perspective, this trust will also be the foundation for further analytics and further marketing as a service, which in turn brings more added value to both customer and company.

So the customer data revolution could cause brand communication's classic relevant sets to disappear. If a crazy market researcher shakes you awake at three in the morning in 10 years' time, his question will not be 'which five brands come to mind first?' but 'which five companies do you allow to use a lot of your personal data?' The entry into the relevant sets will no longer come about through brand recognition and image but through trust and data, which in a world of individualized products and services often determine the quality and benefit of those exact same products and services. The reverse is often also true: if the benefits are right, we will share our data. Our readiness to do so will rise as we realize that analytics is not just used at the surface level of advertising, but is also part of a whole marketing cycle that goes from user-centred product development to after-sales service.

What Is Evil?

Good and evil are not as easy to identify in the complex field of informational self-determination and data-driven marketing as the data protectionist moralizers believe. Let's begin with the digital world's devil incarnate. For a few years now that person has been Eric Schmidt, the man who stole Bill Gates's crown. In December

2009, the then-CEO of Google, normally someone who chooses his words carefully, slipped up when talking to the CNBC television channel. Commenting on the protection of privacy, Schmidt said, 'If you have something that you don't want anyone to know, maybe you shouldn't be doing it in the first place.' In earlier times – at least in democratic societies – such an attitude would only have been expected from the directors of secret services. It means, in effect, that only criminals and other miscreants need the right to a private sphere.[3] It is also an open secret in Silicon Valley that Google's workforce tend not to use Gmail for their private email account, as they know that their employer is reading along with them. That fits wonderfully into the cliché of a 'data monster'.

The next time you are on the Web, type in: www.google.com/ads/ preferences. There, Google shows you in a clear and simple way which interest categories you have been put in, based on your web browser usage. These categories form the basis for the interest-specific 'behavioural ads'. You can also change your areas of inter-est, so that future advertising is based on the preferences you have chosen. This is, of course, an ideal way of letting customers see advertising whose content actually interests them. A click on an 'Opt Out' button in the middle of the page is enough to stop the collection of behaviourally related data needed to derive demo-graphic characteristics.

That might not quite fit the image of the digital world's evil superpower. However, it is part of a general trend on the Internet towards more transparency. In spring 2011, Yahoo! started a pilot project in Europe called 'AdChoices', which goes a step further than

---

3 'Ende der Privatheit – Supermacht Google. Das digitale Imperium macht mobil' ('The end of privacy: Google becomes a superpower. The digital empire goes mobile.'), *Der Spiegel*, 11 January 2010.

Google. Users click on particular ads and see which companies are behind the ad itself and the ad selection, as well as the technical process and information that caused them to be shown to that user. The users have the option of changing their preferences or even of de-activating interest-based advertising completely. In France and the US, there are also self-regulating efforts on the part of the advertising industry to flag up all behavioural ads with a small blue 'i' (for information) under the ad.

The signal sent to the Internet community is clear: companies using target-group-specific advertising need to explain how the target groups were formed and why the individual fell into them. Banks have experienced customers' strong reactions to their credit ratings. Most customers are not angry because they fall into a certain category of risk. Customers with a little economic sense will know that such categorization is necessary for a bank's business. However, they have a right to be angry when they are not given a clear explanation of the criteria behind their credit rating.

The New Data Culture

We need to tell it how it is: the catchphrase 'informational self-determination' is, at least in a narrow interpretation, an illusion. We are not always masters or mistresses of our own data in the digital world. We haven't been for a long time. Pandora's box was opened when digital media came along. In 2009, Facebook founder Mark Zuckerberg got a lot of people hot under the collar when he suggested that the era of privacy was over. Of course, that is as ridiculous as the opposing idea that we could keep control of our own data. Self-determined consumers neither want to shut themselves off behind absolutely impenetrable defences nor find themselves completely visible in an Orwellian world.

Simultaneous to the developments in technology, there will

therefore develop a culture of responsible and collectively acceptable ways to deal with data. All companies that deal with data will
have to respect the rules of this culture. Perhaps in the areas of
online gambling, betting and pornography unethical use of data
will still give some profits. And perhaps services like DateCheck
should be regulated out of existence. For US$15, it provides a
comprehensive dossier about a person, including previous convic-
tions, wealth, family etc. However, whoever works in serious product and service businesses should immediately forget any thoughts
of espionage-like methods. Data protection will make his life hell
and – what is much worse – the mature customer will slam the door
in his face.

Four factors, or control mechanisms, will shape the new data
culture.

1. Regulation

National and supranational legislators such as the European Union
are right now busily patching together all manner of data protection
laws. Until we have one global government (unlikely), this patchwork
law-making is probably the way things will remain. The world's diversity is matched by the diversity of its legal rulings. Globalized data
usage will not change this in any hurry. Serious companies will, of
course, keep to the legal requirements, even when there is often a lack
of enforcement, as is increasingly the case.

The complex legal patchwork means that dealing with the various legal requirements has itself become a database issue for
companies that operate internationally. It certainly is a challenge
for data-driven compliance solutions. For example, IBM chose to
locate its Smarter Commerce Initiative's new data centre for web
analytics and marketing optimization in Germany rather than in
its home country of the US. The press release stated that 'because

Germany makes the most stringent data protection and security demands, IBM has chosen this location in order to offer European customers the highest possible degree of security.'[4] This kind of negative choice is probably an exceptional case. Normally states (or legal areas) have an advantage in terms of location when, on the one hand, they provide adequate protection for privacy without, on the other, suffocating innovative solutions and business models.

The political debate around data protection is currently confusing and contradictory. The political decision-makers often seem to follow a paternalistic European political tradition, as if young people have to be protected from themselves on Facebook. The same politicians also demand the right to 'informational self-determination', which basically means that the adult user decides which personal information about him is stored for what purpose. In general, fixed opt-in and opt-out rules are employed as a one-size-fits-all solution by politicians, for example in the new EU cookie law. This law requires all online users, whether on a smartphone, home computer or tablet, to always accept the use of a new cookie. On every site they visit. Online usage would become an obstacle course. Target-group-specific marketing would have the carpet swiped from under its feet. And many free Internet applications would disappear that the mature user likes to use.

However, we can already see – and we are still at the start of this development – that the method of always and actively giving consent is doomed to fail, regardless of whether it is a sensible political goal to suppress targeting. As consumers we have completely lost track of our opt-ins. We click on the consent boxes as blindly as on the terms and conditions boxes for online retail or when we install software.

---

4 Press release, 19 September 2011.

Exaggerated legal structures do not lead to more justice; they undermine the value of law-making. In democracies, participating members of society, mediated by politicians, determine the basic rules by which everyone plays. It is not the politicians' task to create a new law for every new problem. This thought is nothing new. The French political thinker Montesquieu already formulated it in the following manner in the 18th century: 'If a new law is not absolutely necessary, then it is absolutely necessary not to permit a new law.' Politicians would benefit from placing a little more trust in the wisdom of normal people – especially as a good number of politicians still do not have direct experience of the applications in question.

2. Customer Acceptance

We are in a transition phase for the analytic use of data for commercial purposes. Users themselves do not really know where they draw the line. This does not make things any easier for executives making decisions about customer communication. In future, we will see many applications that test the limits of what is acceptable. Some will be successful and others will be given a bloody nose. There will never be a formula for data-based marketing that can be applied globally. Sensitivities will change. We will probably become more sensitive and careful in some areas, for example when face recognition software is an easily accessible technology allowing any passerby to be recognized with a smartphone. In other areas, and personalized product design and advertising will be two of these areas, we will probably become more relaxed.

We are convinced that customer acceptance will be the most important factor for the success of business models that build on data and analytics.

Users will redefine privacy in the coming years and not allow companies to overstep the mark without punishing them.

Intelligent companies will recognize the trend and harness it, taking away customers' concerns about data misuse through self-regulation and transparency.

As in every relationship, whether of a private or business nature: when your partner tries to understand you better, that increases your feeling of goodwill. If you have the impression that you are being spied on, then the relationship is over.

3. Informational Certification Symbols

Who needs the reams of pages explaining companies' data protection policies? They are there purely to safeguard companies in the jungle of data protection clauses and companies are not keen on all this effort. Almost no consumer is going to look at the detailed explanation, which is a good thing. Apparently it would cost the US economy a staggering $1 billion per day in productivity if all consumers really read the privacy policies of the companies they do business with.[5] The number seems a little high to us. However, it is true that the explanations are only going to get longer as regulations increase.

Certification symbols are one way out. The idea is as widely known as it is simple. Certification symbols on consumer goods reduce complexity. They say 'you can trust this product, it meets the following standards and has been certified independently'. There have been such symbols for 'trusted websites' for a few years now and these have definitely enabled online retailers to build trust. Most consumers would be helped a great deal by less complexity in data protection issues. Increasingly, there will be companies that recognize this and look for customer-centric solutions. The simplest solutions will simply be a stamp that denotes that you can trust a particular

---

5 Kelley, P. G. and J. Bresee, L. F. Cranor and R. Reeder, 'A Nutrition Label for Privacy'. Carnegie Mellon University, 2010.

provider or site. Carnegie Mellon University's researchers have gone further and developed a more differentiated but just as understandable approach – the 'privacy nutrition label'. Recalling the nutrition labels that are required on food in the US to specify its nutritional values (carbohydrate, calories, sugar, fat etc.), websites and social networks would compress their use of personal data in easily understood signs.

In addition, users would have an interface giving a clear oversight of opt-in and opt-out possibilities. Nutritional tables do not, of course, stop everyone from eating too much chocolate. But adopting such an approach would be a practical step towards fulfilling the wish for informational self-determination. It could also form the foundation for software tools that allow individual users to automatically manage their own data protection. Consumers could define their general preferences via such software's privacy settings, stating where they personally draw the line. The software would then determine standard cases and recognize the special cases where the user needed to be asked again or make new decisions.

The important thing is that the new certification symbols would need to learn lessons from other areas such as environmental protection or food: on no account should a confusing plethora of labels be allowed to develop – and the labels would, of course, have to deliver what they promise.

4. Marginal Utility and Inflation

Data collection, storage and processing are becoming less and less expensive. However, as already described in Chapter 2.1, companies always have to calculate the marginal utility and to find out when data-based marketing is worthwhile and when the costs outweigh the added value.

In our projects, we often find that the added expense that the handling of fully fledged personalized data incurs is not viable. Turnover can be grown just as well through the analysis of anonymized customer data. In the project discussed on p.118, we work with anonymized data over a number of retail stages for one of the world's leading IT companies. In both B2B and B2C markets we achieve 15 to 20 per cent buying responses among the addressed customers. The best direct marketing shots cannot hope for higher responses and they are considerably more expensive, partly due to the need to meet data protection guidelines.

In the future, we will also see a gradual decrease in the effectiveness of introducing data-driven marketing, for two reasons. Firstly, companies that were early adopters of innovations that later proved successful will have gained considerable competitive advantage. This creates such high barriers to market entry that the slower companies will find they need not bother trying. That is the case for loyalty cards, as described in Chapter 1.2. Secondly, the saturation effect will impact on customer attention, even for the most effective data marketing applications. When everyone is doing the same thing, the application either becomes a matter of common hygiene or the cost-benefit calculation tips the balance and you would be better off sparing yourself the effort.

In Data We Trust

With the right data, we can today work out what customers want. Of course, we don't always get it completely spot-on, but we're getting better at it. We will only have the right data if we engage customers by keeping to the norms of the new data culture. For commercial users, that means giving customers a better contract. A 'New Deal on Data', as Alex Pentland, the MIT professor with a laboratory for 'reality mining', calls it.

In our view, this new contract needs to be built on four pillars:

1. Data security. All customer data needs to be stored safely. Consumers will not tolerate data leaks caused by hacker attacks, such as the one at Sony in 2011. On the basis of more stringent consumer protection laws, they will sue the company to which they entrusted their data. This creates an additional technical challenge for cloud applications.
2. Transparency. Customers want to know what data is stored for which purpose. They will continue to decline to use services when they feel that data is collected and processed unnecessarily. Intelligent companies will proactively create transparency and make the customer's right to information about his stored data a natural part of customer relationships. Personal online dashboards of saved data could be one technical solution. They would have a clear graphic interface and always be just a log-in away.
3. Added value. For the relevance, frequency and added value of the data analytics to be appropriate, there needs to be recognizable added value for the customer. When there is, he or she will accept added value for the provider.
4. Proportionality. Only such data should be collected and stored that really creates added value. Customers should never feel they are being spied on inappropriately. This will be a great challenge in the area of geodata-based applications and face recognition. We have little experience so far of how people will react to individualized advertising in certain places and/or in certain life situations. Where a person's residence and identity are concerned, consumers will be much more concerned about protecting their data. Most users will not accept that other users mark their presence at real places on digital maps without asking their permission, as used to be possible with the Facebook Places function.

Regulation, certification, customer acceptance and marginal utility will further strengthen these four pillars.

In Data We Trust, or the 'New Deal on Data'

Challenges		Limits
1 Data security		**1** Regulation
2 Transparency including ability to delete data	Successful Marketing 201x	**2** Certification
3 Customer benefit • Relevance • Frequency • Added value		**3** Customer acceptance • Use of what is offered • Provision of information • Sensitivity (regarding 'privacy')
4 Proportionality		**4** Marginal utility

Tim Berners-Lee's invention of the World Wide Web over two decades ago 'freed' data. In a 2008 BBC interview[6] he commented on the issue of personal data saying: 'It's mine – you can't have it.' However, what he said next was his key comment: 'If you want to use it for something, then you have to negotiate with me.'[7] Berners-Lee was always ahead of his time. Sophisticated customers will have a clearer idea the value of their data. They will start to use it as their best bargaining chip and ensure that the user has a share of the utility. In data we trust in order to be more successful marketers. Customers trust in companies that deserve their trust.

---

6 http://news.bbc.co.uk/1/hi/technology/7299875.stm
7 Quoted in 'Ende der Privatheit' ('The end of privacy'), *Der Spiegel*, 11 January 2010.

In a Nutshell

- This decade's marketplace winners will be companies whose analytics and data-based marketing can create clearly recognizable benefits for customers – while acting transparently. Companies using target-group-specific advertising need to explain how the target groups were formed and why the individual fell into them. Users will redefine privacy in the coming years and not allow companies to overstep the mark without punishing them.
- It will be interesting to follow developments for the 'tolerated spies' among the data collectors. At the moment Facebook and Google – the two companies with the most attractive 'data for services' offers – fall into this category. The long-term success of both companies depends on whether they are perceived to be transparent or to be thieving data monsters.
- One of the great opportunities of data-based marketing methods lies in realizing the concept of marketing as a service. The right campaign management tools allow marketing to be perceived as useful. In order for that to happen, the following elements need to be present:
  - Relevance. Communicate with the customer only when it is relevant for him or her.
  - Frequency. Do not communicate too often with customers, even if their segment criteria suggest they are suitable for many campaigns.
  - Added value. Make customers an offer that they would not otherwise receive.
- In many regards, political debate about the relationship between data protection and the commercial use of

personal data is often far from reality. National policies are often trying to regulate things they can no longer regulate. Politics has been overtaken by technical realities and global digital user habits. Good policy regarding data must be differentiated; also bear in mind the importance of digitalization for economic growth.

- The catchphrase 'informational self-determination' is, at least in a narrow interpretation, an illusion. We are not always masters or mistresses of our own data in the digital world. Mark Zuckerberg's thesis about the end of the era of privacy is equally wrong. Self-determined consumers neither want to shut themselves off behind absolutely impenetrable defences nor find themselves completely visible in an Orwellian world.

- In parallel to the developments in technology, there will also develop a culture of responsible and collectively acceptable ways of dealing with data. All companies that deal with data will have to respect the rules of this culture. Otherwise, data protection organizations will make life hell for companies and – what is much worse – the sophisticated customer will slam the door in the face of those companies.

- The complex 'patchwork' of international law means that dealing with the various legal requirements has itself become a database issue for companies that operate in multiple countries. It certainly is a challenge for data-driven compliance solutions. States (or legal areas) have an advantage in terms of location when, on the one hand, they provide adequate protection for privacy without, on the other, suffocating innovative solutions and business models.

- There will never be a formula for data-based marketing that can be applied globally. Sensitivities will change. We will probably become more sensitive and careful in some areas, for example, when face recognition software is an easily accessible technology allowing any passer-by to be recognized with a smartphone. In other areas, and personalized product design and advertising will be two of them, we will probably become more relaxed.
- Most consumers would be helped a great deal by less complexity in data protection issues. Privacy certifications could be a customer-centric solution. It is important that on no account should a confusing plethora of labels be allowed to develop – and the labels have to deliver what they promise.
- We need a 'new deal on data'. The data contract for the digital (consumer) society will be based on four principles:
  - Data security
  - Transparency
  - Customer Benefit
  - Proportionality
- My data belongs to me. If you want to use it, you have to negotiate with me.

Index